Tony Warren

Penguin Books

Understanding Schools as Organizations

Charles Handy is Visiting Professor at the London Business School, a writer and broadcaster and a consultant to a wide variety of organizations in business, government and the voluntary sector.

Born in Dublin, he was educated at Oxford and the Massachusetts Institute of Technology (Sloan School of Management). He has worked for Shell International and as an economist for the Anglo-American Corporation. In 1967 he joined the London Business School to start and direct the Sloan Programme there and to teach managerial psychology and development. He was appointed Professor in 1972. He is the author of *Understanding Organizations* (Penguin 1976), *Gods of Management* (1979), *The Future of Work* (1984) and *The Age Unreason* (1989). He was Chairman of Education for Capability for five years at the RSA where he is now a Vice-President. Charles Handy lives in London and Norfolk with his wife Elizabeth. They have two children.

Robert Aitken has spent his whole working life in the public education service, with breaks only for national service and university. Since 1958 he has worked in educational administration and was Director of Education for Coventry Metropolitan District Council from 1969 to 1989. His particular professional interest is youth, and he has been Chairman of the National Council of Voluntary Youth Services since 1982. He was also Secretary of the Community Education Development Council and a member of the Active Tutorial Work Committee of the Health Education Council. He has studied education systems in the United States, Canada, Sweden, Austria and Russia and has made professional visits to Germany, Romania and China.

D0543623

Company ideology & association /
self actualisation / self esteem

Cultures ⟵ person
club \ role task

structure ———————— different for
different &
functions

core diversity Co-ordination
operating of whole
group
client
| needs
serviced
by "staff"

Charles Handy and Robert Aitken

Understanding Schools

as Organizations

23/9/95

Penguin Books

reactions to
role pressures
filter

compensate
avoid

P23 stakeholders

P38 Pile of purposes
& need to focus

P41/2 role ambiguity
P58-60   & overload

Individual
motivation

needs
hierarchies

goals
(rational
man)

self

Expectancy
of
success
levels

reinf
orcement
of
positive

attrib
ution

lot
fault)

PP63-72 groups

authority

resource position expert personal
charisma

PENGUIN BOOKS

Published by the Penguin Group
Penguin Books Ltd, 27 Wrights Lane, London W8 5TZ, England
Viking Penguin, a division of Penguin Books USA Inc.
375 Hudson Street, New York, New York 10014, USA
Penguin Books Australia Ltd, Ringwood, Victoria, Australia
Penguin Books Canada Ltd, 2801 John Street, Markham, Ontario, Canada L3R 1B4
Penguin Books (NZ) Ltd, 182–190 Wairau Road, Auckland 10, New Zealand

Penguin Books Ltd, Registered Offices: Harmondsworth, Middlesex, England

First published in Pelican Books 1986
Reprinted in Penguin Books 1990
10 9 8 7 6 5 4 3 2 1

Copyright © Charles Handy and Robert Aitken, 1986
All rights reserved

Printed in England by Clays Ltd, St Ives plc
Filmset in Monophoto Times

Except in the United States of America, this book is sold subject
to the condition that it shall not, by way of trade or otherwise, be lent,
re-sold, hired out, or otherwise circulated without the
publisher's prior consent in any form of binding or cover other than
that in which it is published and without a similar condition
including this condition being imposed on the subsequent purchaser

Contents

Introduction 7

1 Organizing Schools 11

2 Are Schools Different? 34

3 Dealing With Individuals and Groups 47

4 Running the Organization 73

5 Facing the Future 102

References and Further Reading 128

Index 131

Introduction

In 1976 Penguin published *Understanding Organizations* by Charles Handy. The book was intended to be a guide to the theories and practices of organizations, to be used by those who were involved in running those organizations or planned one day to do so. It was written with business organizations in mind, and most of the practical illustrations were drawn from that kind of organization, but it nevertheless came to be used across a variety of organizations – in schools, health care, the police and the voluntary sector. It is now in its third edition and is used more widely than ever.

It is reassuring to find that many of the truths about organizations hold good across the board, although perhaps it should not be so surprising since all organizations are, in the end, made up of groups of people. Nevertheless, organizations *do* differ, in their purposes and their priorities, in their traditions and in their language. The very word 'manage' is anathema, for instance, in some places, being thought akin to manipulation, where in others 'hierarchy' or, sometimes, 'democracy' are the forbidden ideas. The theory needs translating for different surroundings.

The practical applications will differ too, even though the theory remains the same. What does 'achievement motivation' imply for teaching practice in the classroom? What does a 'matrix organization' mean when applied to a comprehensive school? What are the sources of power available to a headteacher? They are likely to be different from those that underwrite the position of a managing director of a business. Again, a translation of the theory is needed.

This book is intended to help in that translation, and to provide teachers, and all those concerned with schools, with an introduction to some of the more relevant pieces of organization theory. It is too easy, immersed in the day-to-day pressures of teaching, to forget that a school is also an organization, that teachers are people as well as teachers, that children too are 'adults with L-plates', all with their own motivations, with the same reactions to groups and to authority as the rest of us. Forgetting about organizations it is too easy to think that schools are laws unto themselves; so that while in any other organization people would think that work groups become unwieldly and too impersonal to manage properly if they comprise more than, say, 12 or 15 people, schools are constructed around class sizes of 25 and upwards. Such things are partly a question of resources, of course, but if the assumptions behind the allocation of those resources are not properly understood then the resources become a matter for political argument rather than an organizational necessity. To put it another way, kicking against organizational logic is not the easiest way to run an effective school.

This small book cannot be a comprehensive guide to organization theory. For that the reader is recommended to look at the parent volume, *Understanding Organizations*. Chapters 3 and 4 in this book provide a taste of the style and format of that book with a selection of the key topics. The other chapters set the theory in its context: the school.

Chapter 1 describes the organizational job of the school, at both primary and secondary level. It is a picture that should elicit an echo from any headteacher, as she or he recognizes the dilemmas and delights of their own job in organizational terms; but individual teachers, too, need to see their role in organizational terms, for it will be a key argument of this book that every teacher is also a manager, of a class, with all that that implies. This, in other words, is a book for all teachers, not just for heads.

Chapter 2 examines the ways in which schools *are* different from other organizations and questions whether they need to be quite so different, because the differences cause difficulties. Left to themselves, schools have tended to re-invent their own organizational wheel, but with some interesting deviations and appendages that time has hallowed, so that they are now accepted without question or complaint. For example, schools have grown into large and complex organizations, yet they still rely on part-time management from busy professionals. It might have been possible, even sensible, to run a small school in one's spare time. Is it still sensible with a large one?

Chapter 3, the first of the two theoretical chapters, looks at the theories about *individuals* in organizations, what motivates them, the roles that they get into and the influences of those roles on their behaviour, the way groups work or don't work. These concepts are crucial to all heads who want to understand and organize their staff, but they are also crucial to the teacher as manager – the teacher who needs to understand classroom dynamics, the best way to stimulate individual students and the motivational impact of different types of grading system.

Chapter 4, the second theoretical chapter, looks at the organization as a whole, what kind of culture it is – a private kingdom, for instance, or a bureaucracy? – and the implications of being one or the other. It will look at the sources of influence that are open to teachers: can a head of department *tell* one of their teachers to do something or only *ask* them? It will examine the different sorts of structure that are on offer, and question why the school is organized so much like a traditional production factory and has so little of the product or project flavour of the more successful businesses.

Chapter 5 returns to the practical politics of education and takes a look into the future. Everyone can see that the world of education is changing. What are the problems and, more excitingly, the opportunities for schools? Will falling rolls mean smaller schools, or will the new pressures for education throughout life bring new clients into the schools if they are prepared to receive them? Will new technological devices allow schools to revise their ideas of how and where students study, and if so what does this do to the timetable and the role of the teacher? Will schools be able to meet all the new curricular demands themselves or will they increasingly find themselves part of networks, and what will *that* mean for the role of the head or the style of management?

This book was first published in 1986, well before the Educational Reform Act was born, giving new shape to the curriculum and increased responsibilities to heads and to governors. Nothing in that Act changes anything in this book. Indeed, the Act emphasizes that schools are organizations in their own right, organizations that need to be managed, with heads as their managers. The Act therefore underlines the importance of thinking organizationally as well as educationally, although it does not put it quite as succinctly as that.

Five chapters make a short book. We hope that the reader will want to read further and deeper. The companion volume, *Understanding Organizations*, has a whole section devoted to the supporting literature, while at the end of the present book there is a list of some of the books on organizations and on schools that we have found most helpful.

This book has two authors. Charles Handy, who wrote *Understanding Organizations*, was the principal contributor to the more theoretical sections. Robert Aitken, Director of Education in Coventry, puts the theory in its context of schools and education. It has been an educational experience for both of us, to test our ideas against experience and vice versa. We hope that we may encourage others to test our ideas against their experience and to discover that the school and the classroom, when looked at through organizational spectacles, are extraordinarily interesting places.

Robert Aitken
Coventry

Charles Handy
London

1 Organizing Schools

Schools are also organizations. Sometimes the preoccupation with so many children, with the odds and ends of schooling, with the dramas of young people's lives and all their emotions, can blind one to the fact that all the things are happening within an organization that is itself bound by the laws of other organizations. Box 1.1 shows how it feels, in the words of a primary-school headteacher describing a typical Monday morning in his school.

Box 1.1 Monday morning

I needn't pick up Mrs Churchill this morning. She rang at 7.30 a.m. to say her baby daughter Lisa was ill, and she would have to stay at home to look after her. Funny how calls at 7.30 a.m. at home and 8.30 a.m. at school usually mean some staff emergency!

No work on the stationery requisition today. I will take J2, and the school secretary can rough out stationery requirements after finishing the dinner money. I quite enjoy J2 – a class full of characters, and a challenge. Staff always reckon *I'm happier when I'm teaching*.

Parked at school by 8.10 a.m. As usual three staff have beaten me to it – deputy, head of infants and nursery teacher. Talked over change of plans with Miss Butler, my deputy. Amended day's information in staff diary before she took it to send round staff prior to start of school. Checked with Mrs Griffin, head of infant department, that all was organized for the hair inspection by the District Nurse at 9.30 a.m. Half-past eight has passed – no telephone call. No further staff absence today. *We'll manage.*

Children and parents already paying dinner money at secretary's window. Nursery teacher rings on internal line to say she's discovered three broken windows in her activities room. She will find caretaker. Parent arrives with son – she is taking him for a medical but would I arrange to keep a dinner for him? Secretary passes message to cook. Father arrives to ask would I act as guarantor so that he can buy clothing for children? Agree and sign. What have I let myself in for? Phonecall from professional assistant in Education Department to ask if she could visit school later today to inspect crumbling temporary classroom and state of nursery decoration. Agreed – she knows her way around and staff and children are used to visitors.

Box 1.1 – *contd*

Now to J2 ... but no, a knock on the door, NSPCC inspector from Special Unit to discuss report from a neighbour about a possible non-accidental injury to one of our children. It is urgent I talk to him about it because *we are worried about the child too*. Quick message to Miss Butler – take assembly, please. My assembly on 'Treasures' will have to wait. She will use one of her stock for emergencies. Discussing case – panic – who is registering J2? *Panic over*. Miss North, part-time teacher, passes window with J2 on the way to assembly. I eventually get to J2 at 9.40 a.m.

Monday morning in a primary school!

Box 1.1 captures the atmosphere of school, the pressure of the immediate, the intense involvement with people both inside and outside the school. The emergencies can be of intense personal concern, as with the boy whom the NSPCC inspector wanted to discuss. Always there is the human dimension that is part of the fascination of working in a school; the opportunity to be involved in the daily experiences of people – their frailties and their joys, their values and their growth.

The school in Box 1.1 is one of 20,384 primary schools up and down the country. It has 216 children, aged between 4 and 11. The head has a staff of nine teachers, one of whom is part-time, three nursery assistants, an education assistant to help with the reception and infant classes, a caretaker, five cleaners, a cook and eleven kitchen staff. It is a society in miniature. It is an organization as well as a school.

Any organization needs systems for communicating and arranging things, as well as a structure for dividing up the work and defining the relationship of people to each other. It will require someone to set priorities and define responsibilities and duties. Someone then has to make sure that these responsibilities are carried out and must apportion praise or disapproval when necessary. Without these prior arrangements every problem becomes a crisis, every event something that needs the individual attention of the person at the centre.

The events in Box 1.1 were handled expeditiously and caringly because there was a pre-arranged organization in the school, there were relationships that could be relied upon, and there was support for the school from parents and the wider community. Was this what the head meant when he said, 'We'll manage'? Was he referring to that pre-planned system of organization or did he mean, 'We will cope with these problems. We'll get by'?

Is it only a British habit to use 'manage' in the second, more belittling way, to mean 'coping'? This is to relegate management to a necessary chore, something unnecessary in an ideal world. When the head said, 'I'm happier when I'm teaching', he may also have been reflecting the common feeling among heads that one is a teacher first and always, and a manager by necessity. As we shall see, it is characteristic of professionals to see management as a service function. But professionals do not like to think of themselves as members of an organization, preferring words like 'partnership' or 'practice' or 'consortium'. The dilemma for schools is that willy-nilly they *are* organizations, not just groupings of teachers, and they have to accept that the management of these organizations is a key activity, not a mere service function.

Relegating 'managing' to 'coping' has another disadvantage. It makes it harder for the ordinary teacher to see herself or himself as a manager. Yet it will be a consistent theme of this book that *every* teacher is, properly speaking, a manager of a group of children. The classroom is itself a mini-organization in which all the laws of group behaviour, motivation, leadership, communication and relationships apply. To treat these managerial facets as in some sense trivial compared to 'teaching' not only will make life more difficult for the teacher but may deprive the pupils.

This chapter, then, will look at the different types of school as organizations that have to be managed to be effective.

The primary school

In the opening example the head and his staff were able to deal with the problems that arose because they were able to rely upon:

- the organization of the school;
- the quality of relationships within the school;
- the support of parents and the wider community.

But what, typically, would be the features of a primary school that enabled this? What choices have to be made to decide on the forms of organization? What kind of relationships would be forged? What is the context of support from the community or world outside the organization? How is such an organization to be managed so that it is kept fresh, responsive and effective?

Organization

The first and fundamental step that a head faces (and re-faces each year with changes in children and teachers) is how to *organize* the school. She or he must first decide how to divide the children into learning groups, of what size, age, mix and for what activities, etc.; and then decide how to deploy the skills of the staff to these groups and tasks. The options are many. There is no single answer. In our example the head has chosen to organize his children into seven classes (plus a nursery) of roughly equal size (average twenty-five pupils) according to age; and to allocate each of his full-time teachers to a class, using his part-time teacher and himself to facilitate small-group work or enable teachers to take other classes for special activities. Given the current conventions of British primary education this form of organization is typical of the majority of schools.

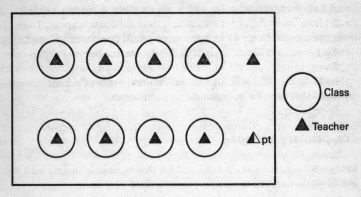

Figure 1

The basic organizational 'chart' could be depicted as in Figure 1. This form of organization makes much sense and has a lot of strengths. It offers security to children and staff alike; they know their place in the order of things. Each class is like a large family with the opportunity during the course of a year to know one another and their teacher well: to know and grow together. The head knows who is responsible for what stage of development. Basic roles are clear. It is an example of what we shall call, later in the book, a 'job-shop' structure, where each unit has its own independent task to do.

Each class group could therefore be depicted as in Figure 2. Yet each class is but a mini-society within the larger society of the whole school,

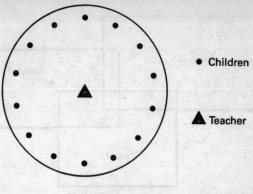

Figure 2

and here complications can set in. Each class is likely to develop or exhibit its own character or culture deriving from the make-up and background of the children in the group and in the person of the teacher (who herself or himself has strengths and weaknesses).

Every society has its own culture, and nothing in education is value-free. Does the class take its values from the teacher or from the group norms or from both? What if eight classes and their teachers go in differing directions? What about the inexperienced or weak teacher? There needs to be some cohesion or conformity for the whole organization, a higher order of things than the class group, if the school is going to be more than a collection of eight different families. How is that to be achieved, and for whom?

In practice the situation is more complex than that. Within the setting of a school there are other groupings, each coming from a different position with differing experiences, expectations and values. Children are different from adults; teachers are different (in their professional role) from parents. These form distinct 'peer groups' in the sense that one takes some of one's values and behaviour from people with a similar background. An alternative expression of such groups within a school could therefore be Figure 3.

There are of course other groups (including the other adults, the non-teaching staff). The caretaker who lives on site is often an influential figure with a foot in both the local community and the school. From their different vantage-points, or *roles*, these people affect and influence what happens in the classroom.

So a primary-school head has a more complex task than just creating

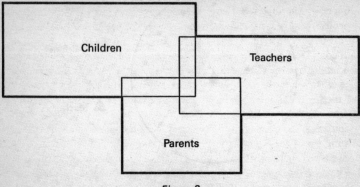

Figure 3

a form of organization. She or he needs to see that the working of that organization is informed by, and recognizes, the influences of other groupings, and to guard against the inadequacies of the organization she or he adopts. This depends a great deal upon the quality of relationships operating within the organization.

Relationships

We have seen that it is one thing for a head to create an organization: yet another to supervise its working. One of the fundamental tasks facing any head is to get the teaching staff to express a collective will. This is necessary because the teacher in her or his own classroom is *the* expression of the school. If discontinuities in the treatment, learning or development of children are to be avoided, then a corporate purpose is needed. Yet teaching is such a personal activity; there is an interactive chemistry between learner and teacher, which depends as much on process as on content (if not more) and expresses personal values and realities as much as knowledge. There is an actor or artist in the make-up of most successful teachers, which sets great store by freedom of expression. This can be at odds with the role of teacher as the expression of the collective purpose or even as manager of the learning group.

But the head needs to ensure that there is an agreed purpose behind the structure of the organization; a shared set of aims, a way of doing things, a means of monitoring progress. This means arriving at a shared set of values and expectations – particularly as schools are inevitably involved in the business of the development and transmission of values.

How then does one combine professional autonomy and artistic freedom with a common purpose? This is the challenge that faces all schools and all professional organizations. In the setting of a primary school a head can do this by various means. She or he may choose to lay down the main content of syllabuses and schemes of work and the methods to be used, and leave the interpretation and pace to the professional competence of each teacher. This, however, is unlikely to be sufficient. Content and methods change and need updating. Even reading schemes can become quickly outdated in a multi-cultural society. The advent of computers in the classroom and the need to identify children with special learning needs are other examples of current changes that require response within the organization.

What is important is that the organization knows its way – where it is going – and that those working in the organization know what it stands for and what are the shared set of values to which each is contributing. To achieve this is not easy. The head will be able to use the expertise of her or his staff by allocating leadership roles in areas of the curriculum, such as mathematics. This can be invigorating for the member of staff involved, releasing and enhancing commitment and motivation. But not all staff are equally experienced or capable of such leadership roles. Minor roles can be felt to be insignificant and demanding. The choosing of staff for responsibilities is a tightrope any head or manager has to walk, particularly if promotion remains the main reward for good teaching, for not all good teachers make good leaders of teachers. Schools, like other organizations, have to find ways to reward good performance that do not involve giving the person a different job.

We shall see later that the size and form of the organization can produce imperatives, forces that can dictate unintended answers and cloud issues. The size of a primary school, with 9 or so teachers and 10 or 12 support staff, should mean that the head and staff are able to communicate personally and frequently, unlike in the larger organizations that many secondary schools are. But smaller organizations are not immune from contrary forces. They may become a dictatorship (owing too much for their purpose to one person) or an oligarchy. Anyone who has lived in a small-scale setting (e.g. on a ship) will know that personality conflict can be a real problem and a divisive influence. Primary schools, despite their apparent 'bonus' of relatively small scale, do not escape the need to face and work at the issue of relationships.

The definition of *roles and responsibilities* and the choosing of staff to undertake them is a crucial task for any head, and it can present difficulties. Even the basic task of allocating teachers to classes can be fraught. Heads sometimes have the difficulty of moving a teacher from, say, top juniors to second-year juniors. There are cases where a teacher has taken the same class in the same classroom for ten or more years. It has become her or his class and rightful empire – impregnable to the rest of the school and sometimes a deadweight in the evolving organization. *Territory* is a prized possession in every organization, with its boundaries fiercely defended.

Roles and responsibilities are important both so that tasks can be undertaken and also because they offer security and a place in the organization for the individual. But this of itself is insufficient. A *collective purpose* is still needed. All members of the organization need the motivation to feel they are partners in it and, particularly for teachers, that they are valued as professional people. Their views need to be heard (and if necessary challenged). This process of achieving a collective view is one of the most difficult tasks – if not *the* most difficult – of a head. It cannot be rushed or taken for granted. It is a continuous process and one that cannot be left to casual conversations or a quick discussion in the staff room at playtime – valuable as those can be. A collective purpose can be achieved only if it is truly collective, i.e. representing the considered views of all involved.

Those involved start, obviously, with the staff, but it goes further than that; parents, families and the community have expectations of, and influence on, the organization. Their confidence in the school is an essential ingredient in its successful functioning. They too have to share in the collective purpose if they are to be truly supportive of the organization.

Parents and the wider community

When parents commit their children to attending primary school they do so with a sense of confidence but also with expectations and fears. Symbolically it is another expression of untying the apron-strings. Their children need to be growing in the company of other children and learning beyond the family under the guidance of specialists. But there can be a sense of loss; the influence of the family can be felt to be waning. Their children will be subjected to other values and knowledge, including those from other children from different backgrounds. This can produce tensions and dependencies of several different orders at times and an increasing need for parents to understand the 'influence' of the school system on them and their families.

So for all schools there is a bond between them and the families and communities they serve. It is a kind of bond of confidence, of trust, that exists between them. Why else does a father ask a head to act as guarantor? And why else is the head really worried about what 'I have let myself in for'?

In practice it is not as simple as that. Some parents are over-anxious, and expect more from the school for their child than is realistic. But sadly too many other parents abdicate once their child is at school. Teachers know that the parents whom they really want to see, to know and to help are often the ones who never come to school. Fortunately the community school movement is changing this and enabling parents, especially those who are nervous of schools and teachers, to have confidence in their role (see Chapter 5, page 119). Whatever the attitudes of parents, this is a critical dimension that the school as an organization has to *manage*, rather than accepting it as part of the scenery. Put in another way, the boundary of the system reaches out beyond the school gates. Organizations are never islands unto themselves.

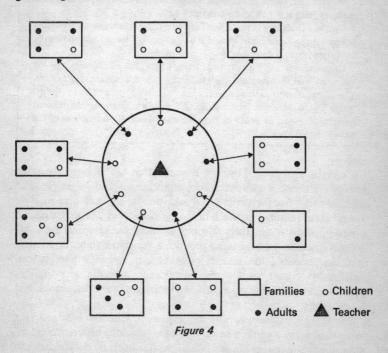

Figure 4

If we take the class group as the basic unit of the school organization, this 'community dimension' can be expressed as in Figure 4. The arrows indicate the flow of cultural forces between school and home.

Box 1.2 Boundaries

One of the key problems in managing organizations is where to set the boundary of the system that you want to influence or manage.

Should railways, for example, think of their world as starting at the railway station or the goods yard? Or should it extend into the home and the office? If the latter, they would find themselves thinking of better home/rail links and might end up in direct competition with buses and taxis. But maybe that's where they should be.

Do a prison's responsibilities cease at the prison gates, or is there some responsibility for the family of the prisoner or for the prisoner after he or she leaves? Or does this fall within the boundaries of other services?

In business, if you confine yourself to making one garment for one large chain store you can be dangerously dependent on one customer and insulated from fashion changes. Prudence might suggest wider boundaries with some direct sales to customers. Efficiency, however, would argue the contrary, that it is best to do one thing well.

Should a voluntary housing relief organization concentrate on providing homes for the homeless or should it also campaign locally and nationally for better housing provision?

Organizations are typically pulled two ways. One pull is to extend the boundary and thus increase one's influence over the constraining factors. The other pull is to concentrate on what you can do best and let the rest go hang. The right compromise is never easy. Organizations can become overstretched just as easily as they become blinkered and victims of the world around them.

It can be seen from Figure 4 how children are in only a relative state of relationship with the school and its ethos and its people. The children come from a variety of backgrounds: e.g. numbers in their family; their position in the family; the quality of life and material provision in the home; their religious or racial background. Such differences in cultural background produce a variety of states of learning from sources outside the school: for example in language development, socialization, 'street wisdom', emotional and intellectual growth. This also produces different patterns of behaviour, attitudes, needs and dependencies.

And these are seldom consistently expressed. Children have differing areas of experience and can be very adept at switching between 'cultures' and using the 'language of the situation' as it suits them. All children can be chameleons! As a result there are strong cultural influences from outside the school that are brought into the classroom daily, but the culture of the school also extends outwards and into the homes of the children. These cultural influences are expressed by the arrows in Figure 4.

So not only has the head of any school the problem of securing continuity in the education of pupils through differing teaching styles of her or his staff. She or he also has a need to secure as much common ground as possible between the school and home 'cultures'. She or he needs to work with the staff for a sufficient understanding between home and school so that what is done at school is not undone at home and vice versa. Thus schools and homes are increasingly readily open to parents and teachers respectively, and many schools are developing as community schools with a curriculum expressed in community/family terms.

Although a primary school may seem to be small and intimate it is in fact a complex and relatively large undertaking or *system*. The *average-sized* school will have 30 or so adults and about 200 children *within the organization*. But, as we have seen, the school is inextricably bound up with the culture of the wider community, particularly that of the parents and families.

The primary school is a significant management task, not only for the head but also for each member of staff, because each has to express the purpose of the school in managing her or his own class. Each and every primary teacher therefore has to be a manager. Every teacher has the task of setting goals and targets for a group, for organizing that group and providing the sources for it, for managing the relationships within the group and the relationships between the members of the group and the other groups or families to which they belong. Every teacher has to decide how to excite and stimulate each individual, what style of behaviour to adopt, what methods of persuasion or influence to use, how to reward and punish, how to handle differences and arguments. Knowledge of one's subject counts for little if one can't do these, which are *all* management functions.

The secondary school

The tasks facing a secondary head teacher are *intrinsically* the same yet even more complex. The functioning of a secondary school similarly depends upon the nature and quality of:

- organization;
- relationships;
- support of the wider community;

and the *inherent* pressures – from both within and without the school – are the same. But *the emphases are different,* and there are additional factors to be accommodated such as:

- size;
- the advancing maturity of the students (including the fact that they have already had seven or so years of schooling);
- the increasing force of peer-group pressures;
- the demands of the examination system;
- employment expectations;
- the approach to adulthood.

The head's palette box has the same primary colours, but the hues are more varied, often more intense but also more subtle. Let us look further at some of these aspects.

Size

There are 4,553 secondary schools in England. They range in size from 45 to 2,001 students. Given a national average pupil-to-teacher staffing ratio of 16.5, this means that the average size of a secondary-school teaching staff is 54. For the larger schools (over 1,200 students) the teaching staff will number more than 80 (including part-timers). There may well be more than 50 other staff.

Secondary schools are therefore large organizations by any standards. In addition to the teaching staff there will be more non-teaching staff, more parents and families and additional outside interests. The spectrum of main interests and influences in the school as an organization could be expressed as in Figure 5. The school has to be organized and managed so as to be able to 'box this compass'. And it has to be remembered that the students who are at the centre of these interests have to box the same compass. The management of the school has therefore to help each student to cope with the influences and values pulling him/her in different directions.

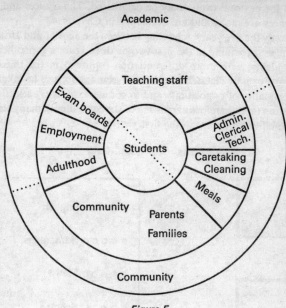

Figure 5

Organization

The tasks facing a secondary head in creating an organization for her or his school are similar to those of a primary head:

- how to organize the students into learning groups;
- of what size, age mix and for what activities and stages;
- how to deploy the teaching and technical staff to these groups and activities;
- how to relate these to the space and facilities available.

The options are many and the answers are many (i.e. as expressed in the variety of forms of organization being practised). The design (or change) of an organization is a question of values. As for any designer, a decision to emphasize this or that feature determines the place and space left for other features. An order of importance – of what is valued in the organization – is created. And the organization goes on expressing those values. If, for example, specialist subject teaching is the prime basis of a school organization, then, as we shall see, other aspects – such as the provision for pastoral care – may be debilitated. The choices and their consequences are many and are developed in Chapter 4.

Commonly the five years' schooling between the ages 11 and 16 is seen as two stages: providing in the first two or three years a general course for all students; with more differentiation (options) in the third and fourth years, usually dictated by choice of examinations to be taken. To maintain equality of opportunity and to counter over-early selection or specialization (and therefore narrowing of the curriculum), many schools adopt all-ability groupings in the first year or so.

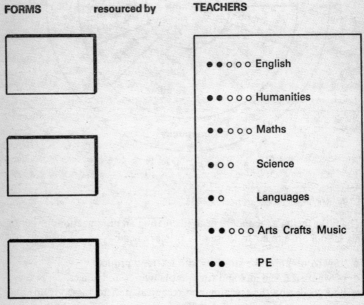

Figure 6

The basic model of the organization of a school with three forms in the first year might be expressed as in Figure 6. This example relates to a small secondary school with about 90 students (three forms of entry) in the first year divided into classes of about equal size (30). The total number of staff (including part-timers) would be between 25 and 30, and some (indicated by ●) would be allocated according to their specialisms to teach first-year class/es. Some may teach more than one subject. For larger schools (e.g. eight forms of entry, 240 students per year) the number of classes would of course be greater, as would be the number of staff. The same model would to a greater or lesser extent express the organization also of the second and third years.

There are obvious strengths and weaknesses in this form of organization:

- the classes offer stability and security to the student groupings;
- the roles and responsibilities of staff are clear;

but:

- the differences of style between seven or so staff teaching the same group can lead to differences of response *between subjects*;
- the differences of style between twelve or so staff teaching the same year group can lead to different responses *between classes in the same year group*.

That is not to say that roles are automatically clear or that different styles or responses can or should be avoided. These are potential consequences of the organization adopted and are likely to need other organizational arrangements (e.g. meetings between all first-year staff under a head of year).

The same features and considerations will apply in the second and third years under this form of organization. In larger schools the scale of the task of co-ordination is bigger, with possibly as many as thirty staff teaching first-year classes.

At the fourth- and fifth-year stage the tasks facing the organization become yet more complex. It is necessary to arrange the teaching groups so as to match the examination courses or projects chosen by the students. Teaching groups therefore tend to be formed in relation to subjects (or groups of subjects), examination levels and syllabuses. There are several consequences of this:

- more student groupings;
- less stability and security in the teaching group;
- tendency towards polarization of values (between subjects and levels of course);
- polarization of expectations;
- greater differences in motivation (among students and staff).

The organization has become more fractured, dispersed and unfocused; place and role in the organization are less clear.

Taking the example again of a 450-student school, the organizational 'chart' of the fourth year might look like Figure 7. The main groups (1–4) are clearly represented. The overlaps indicate regroupings for

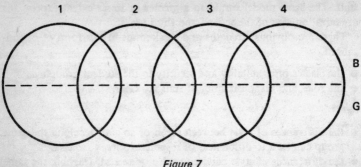

Figure 7

particular subjects, while the dotted line suggests the split between boys and girls for certain activities (e.g. physical education and some crafts). Potentially in this form of organization there are between 12 and 18 different groupings of students. The complexities for a larger school are similar, except in scale.

For the organizational problems of the secondary school intensify in the fourth and fifth year, driven by the demands of academic qualification and subject specialization and the attitudes of students and parents. (The development of Technical and Vocational Education Initiatives, the Certificate of Pre-Vocational Preparation, the new GCSE examination and education for special needs, etc., are adding to these demands.) The school has to work harder to counter the contrary pressures that intensify too. There is a greater need to provide structures within the organization to secure:

● co-ordination,
● continuity;
● commonality of styles and values;
● motivation.

In the language of organization theory, there must be enough *integrating devices* to match the necessary *differentiation*. These are difficulties that face any organization. The larger and more complex the organization the more difficult these nuts are to crack. And, as we have seen, secondary schools as organizations are both large and complex. They need careful and diligent managing if they are not to disintegrate.

The *differentiation* of secondary schools is forced upon them by the subject syllabus and the examination system. The dangers are that the imperative of academic qualification drives out other values cherished by the school, such as according equal respect and opportunity to all students. The reality is less than the ideology. So, for example, attitudes develop among the people within the organization (staff and students) that some subjects are more important than others, that some courses or classes are more valued than others, some teachers, some activities, some students more than others.

Box 1.3 Splitting and binding

Organizations need to specialize their tasks but then need to bond them together. That seems to be an iron law of organizing. But it goes further. The more you specialize the more bonding you need: for every split a binding mechanism.

Lawrence and Lorsch, in the United States, demonstrated that businesses in changing markets or changing technologies had to 'differentiate' their departments if they were not to lose out. The research people had to concentrate on the longer term, for instance, and not get distracted by the short-term fluctuations, whereas the sales force *had* to think short-term and concentrate on today's products and today's technologies. But they also found that those firms who matched the increased 'differentiation' with increased 'integration' devices – such as meetings, liaison groups, full-time co-ordinators, planning teams – were the most effective.

The message, however, is more general than that. Specialists inevitably tend to zero in on their specialism. Someone has to make sure that they are all pointing in the same direction, even if this means compromise for some. It is unwise, and unfair, to leave the end customer, or the student, as the one who has to pull it all together, the final integrator. Unfortunately the co-ordinating and integrating devices cost time and money; they are very visible. Logic says they shouldn't be necessary in a well planned state. Organizational reality says they always are.

As always, what is important is how the organization is perceived by the individual within it. What is his or her place, role, value? It can happen at this stage that some students feel teachers are competing for their time and minds against other subject teachers. It is unfortunately true that many students, particularly those with low or no academic expectations, feel unvalued at this stage. They are not motivated by the organization (except to fulfil its low expectations of them) and are likely to retreat into the security of their peer group, whose anti-school culture becomes stronger than that of the school. When *motivation* and *identity* are lost within an organization, other motivations and identities replace them.

Such dissonances can occur in any organization. Fortunately it often happens that self-adjusting mechanisms begin to operate within the organization. This is more difficult when the style of operation has become habitually engrained or when the organization is subject to strong conditioning by external influences. Change is then a more difficult process and is slow in coming.

This is the snare that secondary schools are caught in to a considerable extent. Academic values and didactic method are deeply engrained, and these are enshrined in an examination system that is based on subject knowledge. Since the examinations are marked against the average of those being examined, only a minority can ever come out top. And since the examinations are designed for only 60 per cent of the age group, there is a large bottom. These largely external factors contribute powerfully to the problems of internal organization that we have described – particularly to the loss of identity and sense of anomie of many students in an organization where such academic values are over-emphasized and other experiences and achievements are under-expressed.

The possibility that individual students could get lost in a large all-ability setting was recognized by the pioneers of the comprehensive school in the early 1950s. They built into the organization a pastoral or house system whereby, for example, a school of 1,200 students had within it an organization of ten houses each of 120 students. Tutors in the houses had responsibility for the welfare, discipline and pastoral care of their groups, including contact with families, the careers service, the courts etc. But, in the language of Chapter 4, it was not always clear whether the pastoral system was 'line' or 'staff', whether it was in charge or advisory.

This system of pastoral care has provided a strong integrating mechanism to counterbalance the disintegrating tendencies in a strongly emphasized academic structure. In addition to attention to matters of general welfare for the group it has enabled face-to-face counselling for individuals. But the pastoral care organization has been under strain in recent years, especially since the school-leaving age was raised to sixteen in 1973 and in the face of developments in society including unemployment. In many schools the provision for pastoral care is as yet only 'bolted on' to the academic framework and accorded only one or two tutor-group periods per week. The adequacy and effectiveness of this are under question.

More recent developments in the pastoral care movement seek a more fundamental synthesis in their approach. They seek to acknowledge and use the resources of the peer group as a positive force in their own education. The main features of this for students are that they:

- work in tutor groups;
- learn by active and experiential methods;
- evaluate their own and the group's performance;
- have more determination of their own development.

Students, in other words, are being asked to learn by working in the kind of task groups that are part and parcel of work in the world outside. This requires a considerable shift of stance and method by teachers. They need to develop skills in group processes; to become enablers rather than instructors; to facilitate learning at first hand (through experience) rather than at second hand (by gathering others' knowledge). They need, in short, to become managers.

This is an example of a self-adjusting mechanism in operation: of positive organic growth within the secondary-school system to cope with a particularly difficult aspect of internal organization. But such changes are not easily achieved. They threaten many established positions and practice. In those schools where this approach is more fully developed, *all* staff have a tutorial role, and learning in academic subjects is based on tutor-group processes. You cannot change the structure and the mechanisms of the school without affecting the roles, relationships, attitudes and skills of the people involved. Educational change inevitably involves an organizational shift, which has to be understood, planned for and managed.

Relationships

This example of 'tension' within a school organization – in this case between the academic and pastoral aspects – throws up many issues of *internal relationships*. There is the need to maintain some commonality of will, style and understanding in all the expressions of the organization, as well as continuity in the education and consistency of treatment of students and in the development of staff. The *issues* are intrinsically the same as for primary schools but more complex because of the nature and size of secondary schools. Because of this they are likely to require substructures within the organization and some means of co-ordinating those structures.

Heads know how time-consuming and challenging this task of

'corporate management' – for that is what it is – can be. They leave their
deputies and heads of faculty to share the responsibility, and the skills
and experience of heads of department and pastoral heads. But, even
more than in a primary school, factions and differences of values have to
be faced. The definition of roles and responsibilities, the choosing of
personalities, the vesting of authority and the creation of time and space
for the exercise of responsibility are all essential ingredients of this pie.

But, again, that is not all; the senior management is not the whole
organization. The contribution and attitude of the 'ordinary' member of
staff need to be recognized, especially in a professional organization.
The teacher in the classroom is the embodiment of the school. A wise
head therefore values and creates space for 'hearing the voice' of ordinary
members of staff, whether individually or collectively through trade
union representation. Indeed, the trade-union angle is probably one that
is under-valued, as a positive force, in school management.

Similarly the *external relationships* are more complex. There is still the
need to recognize the 'bond' with the families of the students, including
the aspirations of parents as their offspring approach occupational
choices. But increasingly the students are reaching out beyond the family
and the school and developing their own interests and aspirations.
Adolescence can be described as a period of apprenticeship to adulthood.
And this is likely to include experimenting with drink, drugs, sex,
smoking, fashions and music, some of which may be stimulated by
commercial pressures. The 'cultures' of home and school are themselves
under pressure from the current youth culture.

There are two more formal external pressures. As the period of
compulsory schooling approaches its end, students as individuals have
to face the prospect (or lack of it) of employment. What kind of job or
career to follow? What are the requirements of employers? What does
'going out to work' mean? What does it mean in terms of a particular
occupation? This interfaces with the requirements of examining boards:
not only GCSE, but also City and Guilds, Tec/Bec and RSA.

These are all issues that the secondary school has to address. They are
points of contact or external relationships they have to maintain. They
are the constituencies of the organization, each one with different expectations of the school. And they need to find expression within the
structure of the organization. The boundary of the school never stops at
the gate.

The school and society

Schools are one of society's key devices for adapting to the future. As such they find themselves mirroring many of the tensions in society, for instance:

Accountability. The school is accountable to the board of governors, which must include parent, staff and community representatives. But schools are also now required to publish annually a prospectus of their curriculum, options, activities and examination results. This gives parents more information to choose between schools, which they are now formally encouraged to do. In effect, the gate to the secret garden of the curriculum and the internal organization has been opened, making the leadership of the school more open to question, both within and without. This mirrors the increased pressure on all public bodies to demonstrate that they are delivering what they ought to deliver.

But the accountability remains confused. Schools are accountable to the profession, to the parents and their children and to employers. Their interests are not always the same, nor are there easy ways of resolving any differences. Schools, like other organizations, will have to find better ways to debate and deal with these confused accountabilities.

Falling rolls. The high birth rates of the 1960s had dropped by up to 30 per cent by the end of the 1970s and have only recently begun to rise again. As a result school systems, after twenty or more years of rapid expansion, are in a period of prolonged contraction, which is likely to extend well into the 1990s.

Expansion within a system provides opportunities for creativity, experimentation, new ideas, rapid promotion. There is the stimulus of a natural yeast working within the environment. Contraction has the opposite results: closures or amalgamations of plants, redundancy or redeployment of staff, fewer opportunities for experiment or promotion. This has a dulling effect, leading to fewer risks and greater caution.

In other spheres they talk of contracting markets rather than falling rolls, but the effects are the same. Leadership has to do its best to counter the ill effects. It means working harder at the infrastructure tasks of providing opportunities for development and fulfilment, of maintaining commitment and motivation – the management tasks. It also means taking another look at the boundaries of the system in case there are opportunities in new markets. The temptation in a falling market is to retrench, but a falling market in one area often suggests that there is a rising market elsewhere. Leadership needs to look out as well as in.

Falling rolls necessarily mean falling spending on education. Money will not be available to fund the kind of slack in organizations that provides the time for development, experiment and special projects as well as the cover for inefficiency. The necessary slack for innovation can be provided in the future only by getting rid of the inefficiencies, by the kind of inspired leadership that raises energy, reduces absenteeism, converts time into effort: by better management, in fact. Without that kind of better management as the substitute for money, the education of our young will be damaged just when it needs more than ever to be experimental and responsive to a changing society.

Summary

Schools are complex organizations; that has been the central message of this chapter. They are more difficult, perhaps, and more complex than other organizations because of the expectations laid upon them and because of the critical place that they have in our society. They have a daunting task. They struggle to reconcile many competing and often contradictory forces without any predetermined structure. That they succeed so often is a testament to the integrity and capability of those who lead them.

Yet it is clear that the management of schools is becoming more difficult. Societal change is accelerating – technologically, culturally, structurally. The general level of education and of expectation in the population is rising. How to respond to these pressures and to manage the changes is the increasing challenge for schools.

But schools are not that different as organizations; that has been the other message of this chapter. The context may differ, but similar issues have to be faced in other organizations. Along with other organizations schools have to:

- Decide on their key tasks, and the constituencies that they serve (the *Strategy*).
- Divide up the work to be done (the *Structure*).
- Find ways of monitoring what is going on (the *System*).
- Recruit the right people and keep them excited and committed (the *Staff*).
- Train and develop them in the competences required (the *Skills*).

- Work out the best way to lead and relate to the people (the *Style*).
- Above all, create a sense of mission and a common set of beliefs (*Shared values*).

These are the seven *S*'s that are commonly regarded as the conceptual framework for organizing, a check-list for leaders (see, for instance, Peters and Waterman, *In Search of Excellence*). To put it another way, schools, just like other organizations, need to:

- define their role and their specific contribution;
- deal with individuals and groups;
- run the organization;
- face the future.

These are the questions that will be faced by the next four chapters in this book. The chapters do not provide the answers but outline a way of thinking about the issues and set out some of the options.

2 Are Schools Different?

Chapter 1 ended by declaring that, in the essentials, schools were just like other organizations. If they are, then it becomes appropriate to learn from those organizations and to apply the theories and findings of organizational research to the running of schools. Schools, however, and schoolteachers have instinctively felt that they were different, if not unique, and needed their own set of theories and precepts. Which view is right?

The answer has to be that both are. In that they are collections of individuals brought together for a purpose, schools are subject to all the problems, limitations and excitements that are inherent in getting people to work together, wherever they do it. But schools are not businesses – it might be simpler if they were – and many of the organizational concepts were hammered out and tested in business organizations. It is important, therefore, to be clear about the differences as well as the similarities so that one can know what to query as well as what to accept in the concepts.

It is important for another reason too. Those who work in schools are used to them; they accept their ways as inevitable – like the weather, pleasant or troublesome, you have to live with it. The differences, however, may not all be inevitable; some may be inherited, some accidental. Since most of the differences tend to make schools more difficult to run, it is crucial that we sort out whether the differences are necessary or not. This chapter will therefore examine four of the principal differences, which could be called:

- 'No time for management'.
- 'The pile of purposes'.
- 'Role-switching'.
- 'The children'.

It is another way of tackling that elusive quest: the role of the school. To compare yourself with others is often the best way to begin to understand yourself.

'No time for management'

This phrase has both a literal and a metaphorical meaning. The most noticeable aspect of a school to anyone arriving from another organization is the absence of offices. There are a few, of course, in the administration area, for the head, the deputies and the secretaries, but where do all the other 'managers' reside – the year heads or house heads, the heads of faculties or of committees? They are, you are told, in class, teaching. Some have a poky little box, but for most their office is their locker, or pigeon-hole, their classroom desk, or the briefcase brought home in the evening. And meetings – the meetings that take up 60 per cent of the time of senior managers in large organizations – when do they happen? On Wednesday afternoons, you are told, after school, at lunch-time, in break or before 9.00 a.m., when the staff are not teaching, in what many teachers see as their own time. There is literally not much time for management.

The lack of managerial offices, of meeting-rooms and meetings is the outward and visible sign of a noticeable feature of school organizations. They try to make do with as little management, in time and people, as possible. Conventional management thinking separates jobs into 'managerial' and 'operational' components. Everyone has some of each, but typically, the higher you rise in an organization the greater the proportion of the managerial element in your life. All managers will have been an operator once, an accountant or an engineer, a sales representative or a clerk, but these operational elements are only very occasionally needed when they move into management roles. Most teachers, on the other hand, would like to concentrate on teaching and keep the managerial element to a minimum if they could. Management is seen as a chore; good organizations should need very little of it (the metaphorical meaning).

Teaching, after all, is what they are supposed to do. The staffing calculations made by local education authorities assume that all teachers have a teaching timetable; indeed, reasonably sized teaching groups are feasible only if this is so, given that children must at all times be under the control of a teacher. Even the teacher's contract, which strangely has never been defined precisely in Britain, leaves non-teaching work to the professional conscience of the individual. Houghton, in his 1974 report on teachers' pay, expressed the pious hope that most teachers would recognize this, but still left it as a pious hope.

This is all very different from other organizations. Consider the following analysis of a manager's job.

Box 2.1 Managers' lives

Rosemary Stewart studied 160 senior and middle managers in British organizations (not schools) for four weeks. This is part of what she found, and other studies suggest that it is not untypical of most managers' lives:

The managers averaged forty-two hours of work per week. *Sixty per cent* of their time was spent in discussion: 43 per cent informal, 7 per cent committee, 6 per cent telephoning and 4 per cent social activity.

Thirty-four per cent of their time was spent alone, 25 per cent with their immediate subordinate, 8 per cent with their superiors and 30 per cent with peers and others. (The numbers are arithmetic averages.)

Fragmentation in work was great. In four weeks the managers averaged only nine periods of thirty minutes or more in a week without interruption. They averaged 12 fleeting contacts (i.e. less than five minutes) per day; they averaged another 13 other contacts to make a total of 25 per day. It would be hard to fit a teaching load into that sort of life.

Geoffrey Lyons, when he looked at the day of headteachers and deputies, found that their life was much the same as Rosemary Stewart's managers. But other organizations have *layers* of full-time managers, while schools have two or three at the top and a few others as *part of their job*. Teachers are teachers first and managers when they have to be, because managing is clearly a disruptive occupation if you have something else to do. There is little time for management in a school. There are, however, only two known ways to run an organization without much time spent on management: by *autocracy* or by *autonomy*.

Autocracy puts the managerial task on to one desk – the head's. If the head takes all decisions and assumes all responsibility, then the time of others is released for teaching. The autocracy can be personal and charismatic or it can be exercised more formally, through rules, procedures and regulations, a school handbook. In both cases it is one person 'managing' while others work. It is the conventional outside view of what a head does.

Autonomy, on the other hand, tries to dispense with the need for management by dividing the work into self-contained units and then letting those units get on with it. There should be the minimum of interdependence or overlap between the units so that co-ordination is unnecessary. If each person does his or her own work in their own shed you can get the co-ordination and joint planning done over coffee.

These are well tried management methods. They are valid methods, *but*:

- Both depend crucially on selection. A bad autocrat or a bad autonomous teacher can cause a lot of damage in these systems.
- Both require small systems to be effective. Realistically, autocracy loses touch if there are more than 15 to 20 subordinates, degenerating into dictatorship, while more than 15 autonomous beings lose cohesion and drift into anarchy.
- Both run the risk of degenerating – into a dictatorship in the case of autocracy, and into anarchy in the case of autonomy – *if the relationships, stressed in Chapter 1, are neglected.*

Autocracy or autonomy might therefore be a viable method in primary schools, *provided* the right people are there in the first place, because they are small enough, the systems are minimal and the tasks relatively independent. Secondary comprehensive or community schools are different. The size of the operation, the necessity for all the independent teaching activities to be also linked together and co-ordinated and the resulting complexity of the whole thing require complicated systems, plenty of 'admin' and a proper middle-management structure. They have to have a requisite amount of bureaucracy, or what we shall define in Chapter 4 as a 'role culture'.

If you try to run a bureaucracy, which is a logical pyramid of jobs, by autocracy you end up by overloading the top of the pyramid. All decisions drift up to the top, where there is no time to take them properly. Because the head and the deputies are the only people with any discretionary time they can end up doing all the odd jobs, picking up little pieces and running messages. In the end they may do all the detailed administration 'to free the others to teach', so that you have the ironic situation of a senior teacher, even a deputy head, arranging bus trips and the layout of an examination hall – activities that in any other organization would be the task of an administrative assistant. The alternative to the 'head as tyrant' can be the 'head as servant' – seldom the 'head as leader' (there is not time for that). The 'servant' role, however, is more to do with holding the organization together than directing it; it is also a recipe for overwork, stress and breakdown at the top, as well as frustrations and backlogs lower down, because all decisions have to go up the pyramid and then down again. Given so little time for management, it is hard to be the 'wise head' of Chapter 1 who hears and listens to the voices of the individual teachers. Given the concentration and scarcity of management time, it is hard for that individual teacher to get involved as much as she or he might want to in the running of the school.

Secondary schools sometimes seem to have inherited the managerial traditions, and the staffing ratios, appropriate to smaller and simpler places. They are trying to run large and complex organizations in their spare time. It can't be done – not with any hope of success. Something has to give: the staffing ratios, the class size, the head's sanity or, in the end, the quality of the output.

'The pile of purposes'

Organizations that have one clear-cut task to do are easy to run. A one-product business may be financially risky but it is not organizationally complicated. All its energies and resources go in one direction; success is clearly measured, and failure is obvious.

Schools are not so fortunate. 'Education' is an envelope word – we can make it include almost anything we want, and schools can end up at the receiving end of all of society's expectations. Success in education is elusive, hard to measure and, maybe, not evident until many years have passed. The following phrases from the 1944 Education Act indicate the very general nature of the official aims of education:

- 'to contribute towards the spiritual, mental, moral and physical development of the community';
- 'to meet the needs of the population of their area';
- to provide 'education suitable to the requirements of junior/senior pupils';
- to provide 'such variety of instruction and training as may be desirable in view of their different ages, abilities and aptitudes';
- to offer 'further education ... [for those] able and willing to profit from the facilities provided'.

This is an invitation, in practice, to do what you please, or alternatively to try to please everyone. That is unsatisfactory enough, but schools have acquired other functions, which are not listed in these aims:

- Custodial – to look after children; if they are young so that their parents can work, if they are older so that they stay off the streets and the dole queues.
- Certificating – to ensure that as many children as possible leave school with some sort of certificate (in the face of a norm-referenced system of examinations, which means that they can't do it for everyone no matter how hard they try).

● Socializing – to encourage in young people standards of morality and behaviour, values and beliefs (the hidden curriculum) that society would like to see in its children, although it may not practise them in the home or in public.

It could be, and has been, argued that these three functions are in conflict with the more developmental aims of education that are officially talked about. It is hard to be friend, judge and guard-dog at the same time. Businesses too have conflicting aims – to make money for the shareholders, to pay more to the workers, to reduce the price to the customers – but in theory it is possible to give more to everyone if the cake grows fast enough. Also, there is at least one common dimension to the dilemma: money; so that trade-offs can be calculated and talked about. Schools, however, as we have seen in Chapter 1, are supposed to 'box the compass' of all the interests invested in them, a compass with at least ten different constituencies often pulling in different directions.

Faced with conflicting functions and no simple way of measuring success, schools have a major management problem. Without clear and agreed objectives there are no criteria for deciding how to allocate re-sources; everything becomes a political debate about priorities. Without clear measures of success there are no obvious ways to assess the progress of individuals and departments; every judgement is subjective and per-sonal. If a school is supposed to please everyone, then everyone has a right to influence every decision. Management gets bogged down in talk.

One way out of this dilemma is to play it all ways. Success is effectively not failing; satisficing becomes a way of life. 'Given the catchment area, we do as well as can be expected' (when it is not known or worked out what could be expected); or 'We pride ourselves on being a very caring school' (when caring for what is unspecified). Where there are no standards it is enough to try hard at whatever you can. If at the end of the day the school has functioned without catastrophe, well at least it has not failed. 'I managed OK today' means 'I coped today' (see Box 1.1, page 11).

Another alternative can be to pick on óne of the few measurable criteria – the 'three *R*'s' in primary school or O-levels in secondaries. Teachers are, however, guiltily aware that they are then in danger of neglecting some of their other aims and functions, of concentrating on one part of their 'compass' to the exclusion of the rest. Guilt can be the unintended legacy of confused criteria.

It may not be the fault of the schools that they are the repositories of society's hopes and fears, whims and fancies; but it compounds the problems of management, turning the practical into the political, the objective decision into the personal opinion, the committee into a debating chamber and the organization into a microcosm of society. It is yet another invitation to autocracy as the only alternative to anarchy, the only way of imposing some direction on that swarm of humanity that is your school. Tempting though it may be, autocracy amid such a confusion of possible purposes is dangerous, particularly when the autocrat has guaranteed tenure. Suppose she or he chooses the wrong purpose to emphasize? It takes time for the neglected constituencies to respond. In a democratic society schools can look strangely feudal to the outsider.

The other response to multiple purposes is to stitch on more bits to cope with more purposes. The pastoral organization, discussed in Chapter 1, could be a piece of organic growth or a 'bolted-on' device. Too many bolted-on devices and the school begins to look more like a kitchen utensil-rack than an organization, with a device for every purpose but no menu for the meal.

Box 2.2 The over-arching goal

In their work with leading businesses David Bradford and Alan Cohen were impressed by the importance of an over-arching goal for an organization. It builds, they say, a common frame of reference that allows people with different backgrounds and specialisms to pull together towards the same end. It is key to any change because it describes what *could* be. It is also highly motivational because it puts individual tasks in a larger framework, giving them point.

An effective over-arching goal has four characteristics:

- The goal reflects the *core purpose* of the organization. The purpose must be the task to be done, not some well meant aim to be the best school in town.
- The goal is feasible. It must be within the grasp of the organization and within the time-span of the key actors, and must be stated sufficiently precisely so that it can be recognized when it is reached.
- The goal is challenging. It must move people forward to a higher level or ranking. People are motivated by having something to strive for, provided it is feasible.
- The goal has larger significance. It must have meaning or importance for others besides the people directly concerned. Great organizations have purposes that reach beyond themselves.

Box **2.2** – *contd*

Above all, however, is the fact that there is *one goal*, which sums up the point of everyone's endeavours.

David Bradford and Alan Cohen, *Managing for Excellence*, Wiley, 1984.

'Role-switching'

The assumption behind the promotion structure in schools is that the best teachers make the best managers. Career success means moving upwards to an increasingly managerial role. Schools also assume, confidently, that a member of their staff can move from being an expert in the classroom to being a representative of the school to the surrounding community to being counsellor to the struggling. It is part of the excitement and richness of the job, of course, but it does make the place more difficult to run if you have to assume that a good teacher is good at everything else.

Other organizations know that a great sales representative is often a disastrous sales manager, that the research chemist may be a great chemist but a terrible organizer; in short, that organizations need to match skills to tasks and that having one skill does not necessarily mean that you have the others. Schools know this too, but their tradition of organizing requires that they try to forget it.

Consider for instance the job of a manager. It is very fragmented. (Mintzberg found that over half of a manager's activities lasted less than nine minutes. Guest found that foremen in a factory dealt with 583 incidents each day. Stewart's managers, as we saw, achieved only nine periods in a week of more than half an hour without interruption.) Mintzberg concluded that 'to be superficial is, no doubt, an occupational hazard of managerial work'; but, he decided, that is what managers thrive on. It is the thrill of keeping several balls in the air; of spurring others on, *not* doing it yourself; of activity, *not* contemplation; of people, *not* words and numbers – these are the essence of management. Not everyone can do it. The loner, the craftsman, the academic, the introvert and the lazy will find their talents unrewarded, even unneeded, in most management tasks. Does management come naturally to a professional teacher?

Professional organizations leave their good professionals alone. They hire others to do the administration but they don't call them 'managers', nor do they put them over the professionals. They call them 'bursars', 'chief clerks' or 'administrators' and regard them as the servants of the professionals, who retain the higher status and the leadership (as opposed to the administration) of the organizations. We shall look more closely at the professional organization in Chapter 4.

Do schools take management talent for granted, assuming that it comes as naturally as driving a car to any competent educated person? Or are they making a deeper assumption, that a good teacher *has* to be a good manager? This latter assumption is actually at the heart of this book, where we take the view that the education and development of a group of children are properly a *management* job not a *communications* job or even an *academic* job. If schools really believed this, there would be considerable justification for all the role-switching that goes on, but they would also distinguish more than they do between the good teacher and the good subject specialist, and would promote the former rather than the latter. It is our suspicion that management ability is more often taken for granted, that management is seen as a reward for climbing the ladder of subject expertise and that schools have been too ready to imitate, unquestioningly, the management hierarchies of business rather than the twin hierarchies of leadership and administration in the professions.

If teachers *are* thought of, and behave like, specialists and academics rather than class managers, then not only will the organization tend to end up with some bad managers (who were good specialists) and neglect some good managers (who are poor academics and therefore unpromoted). In addition, teachers themselves will suffer from 'role ambiguity' as they move from one role to another, often taking on three or four different roles in the course of one day.

We know that role ambiguity is a major cause of stress. If we don't know who or what we are supposed to be in a situation it can be unnerving. We have, however, instinctive ways of protecting ourselves against the unpleasant aspects of stress. The most obvious strategy is to refuse to switch roles. Once a teacher, always and only a teacher. But there are other strategies (see Box 2.3).

Box 2.3 Ways to reduce ambiguity

- Reduce other ambiguities, e.g. think in black-and-white terms, use stereotypes, concentrate on the short term, develop unchanging rules and routines.
- Boost your self-confidence, e.g. find some lesser beings, develop your own territory where you can rule, escape into fantasy through drink or other aids, become aggressive over small matters.

Box 2.3 – *contd*

- Avoid too much exposure, e.g. refuse assignments to committees or other duties, become apathetic and withdrawn, shun social and outside contacts.

The unusual amount of role-switching required of a teacher must make schools difficult places for teachers sometimes. Inevitably, some of the negative responses to role transition will surface from time to time. Inevitably, too, not all those who are called 'heads' (of departments, years or schools) will be the best of managers. Schools are different, but maybe they need not be *so* different.

'The children'

In the end the most distinguishing feature of schools is perhaps nothing to do with roles, criteria or the place of management, but the children. Who are they? What are they? How do they fit into the organization? Hospitals and prisons share with schools this dilemma of a population within a population, but it is not a problem encountered by other organizations, and therefore there are not too many answers or analogies available to schools. When asked how many people there are in the organization, most teachers reply by giving the number of staff. The children are not intuitively seen as members of the organization!

The children are a dilemma because it is not clear how they relate to the organization. It is a dilemma that teachers baulk at, perhaps because they have lived with it so long that it is no longer a problem. 'What do you mean?' they say. 'They are the whole *point* of the school, the reason for our existence, the purpose in our lives.' Quite so, but that does not answer the question. To put the dilemma in the terms of another type of organization:

Are the children *workers*, *clients* or *products*?

The words may shock but they distinguish between three different ways of relating to an organization:

- A *worker* is a member of the organization, who co-operates in a joint endeavour.
- A *client* is a beneficiary of the organization, who is served by the endeavour.
- A *product* is the output, which is shaped and developed by the organization.

No doubt a child is in some ways all of these, but which predominates in a particular school?

One of the puzzling features of British education to the outsider is the abrupt and immense transition that happens to a child at the age of 11 or 12. From the small, personal and holistic world of the primary school he or she passes to the huge, more impersonal and fragmented world of the secondary school for five years, until the world grows smaller and more personal again in the sixth form or further education college. Does it have to be this way?

It appears that the child is being viewed differently at each stage – perhaps for valid educational reasons, but with big organizational implications. The organization of the typical *primary school* is consistent with the view of child as worker. They are grouped together in one place under one supervisor and co-operate with each other, in pairs or small groups, in completing tasks: a sort of workers' co-operative in the best cases. The average *sixth form* is consistent, on the other hand, with the view of the student as client and the school as provider of resources. He or she is allowed to choose from a wide range of services and is encouraged to be independent and self-directing.

The *secondary school*, up to age sixteen, is different. The individual student works for perhaps ten different supervisors (teachers) in one week, in maybe ten different locations, with perhaps three different work groups. There is no one place he or she can call his/her own, even personal belongings being carried round in case or satchel. Sometimes the social (pastoral) group differs from the work group. Co-operation is discouraged, and tasks are highly individualized.

Anyone who had to organize an office or a factory like this would rightly be judged insane. They are conditions designed to produce confused identities, anomie and powerlessness. From an organizational point of view anyone who can produce genuine learning and self-development in such conditions is greatly to be admired. The situation is perfectly logical, however, if the student is seen as a product in the making, moving from specialist process to specialist process in batches of differing quality, graded and inspected individually. Lesson-change to a visitor to a secondary school looks like rush hour or, dare it be suggested, a production system gone frantic.

This may well be an unnecessarily cruel picture of a secondary school. The alternative view would see every teacher, or at least every form tutor, as a manager – of the students. The percentage of managers is not then far away from the standard for other large organizations – if, that is, the students are seen as members of the organization. This approach is not just a convenient way of re-jigging the managerial numbers; it suggests a particular slant to the educational process and requires teachers to see themselves as part of a managed process, with all the accompanying paraphernalia of meetings, records and controls that go with a managed institution of perhaps a thousand people. The missing offices are then the classrooms, which are the territories of the educational foremen – our teachers and their groups of student/workers.

Schools are different because of the children. It makes a vast difference whether teachers see themselves as independent professionals with clients, as managers of groups of co-operating workers or as shapers of products in the making. To claim to be one and then inadvertently to act the other turns schools into pretences where reality undermines idealism. Teachers often have a deep moral and personal commitment to their pupils; it would shock many of them to hear these spoken of as 'products' and to be told that, organizationally, the process of their school was akin to an old-fashioned factory. Actions, however, override rhetoric; the way we organize our schools, particularly our secondary schools, dictates the way the child sees the teacher. *It is as important to understand organizations as it is to understand children or to know your subject.*

Schools are obviously different – and more complex. A school is not a business, but it is important for a school to work out what kind of a business it is in order to make the complexity manageable. That paradox is one message from this chapter.

A school has to decide what kind of organization it is (a factory, a work community, a market-place?), who its customers are, what they want and how that is to be delivered and measured. If the students are *workers*, for instance, not raw material, then it makes sense to ask what products they ought to be producing and for whom; it is possible to work back from this to a process for delivering those products. There is no reason at all why an organization should not be serving a *range* of markets with a *range* of products as long as this is deliberate and not accidental.

The second message from this chapter is that assumptions about the way things should be run and organized have a major effect on the way people see themselves, the way they behave, think and react. Even if the assumptions are unwitting or unconscious and have been around as long as the scenery, they are still potent. Anyone who is charged with running classes, sections of schools or whole schools needs to be aware of what those assumptions are and of their effects. The next two chapters examine these for some of the more important areas of organizations.

Box 2.4 The organizational idea

People seem to carry around with them a deep-seated and often unconscious idea of what an organization is and how it works. Often this has something to do with their earliest experiences of organizations. In the period after the Second World War, military or naval models of organization were prevalent. Most males had spent part of their formative years in the armed services, and it was natural that they should carry over to other organizations ideas about unquestioning obedience, of line commanders and staff officers.

Many parts of the voluntary sector started off as offshoots of the churches. It is understandable that they should model their organization on the local church, with its focal person – the priest – and groups of helpers, shunning any thoughts of hierarchy, precise objectives or tight control procedures. Other voluntary bodies are sometimes presided over by women whose main experience of organizing was the family. Families are difficult to organize, and the woman can often find herself literally managing everything simultaneously, in a pivotal role. Carrying that behaviour over into another organization soon earns one the reputation of dictator.

Where do teachers learn their organizational idea? Conceivably in schools. This, if true, would make schools very resistant to change, if no one has any other ideas as to how the place could be.

---

3 Dealing With Individuals and Groups

There is a certain pleasing conceit among most of us that any sensible person can handle individuals or groups if they need to. Thus it is that people are launched into being parents with no warning or training and into management with a similar careless confidence. No doubt, having ourselves been children, and as individuals and members of groups, we can be expected to know all about it. In fact, of course, the vagaries of human nature, our urges and inclinations, our defences and fears, our reactions to other people and to authority, all combine to make dealing with people the most puzzling and difficult thing to do in life, whether we do it as parents or as teachers, as leaders, or as managers or heads of this and that.

Anyone who has to deal with other people, in whatever capacity, knows that they have to make some assumptions about:

- *individuals as individuals*: what each person wants or expects out of life and out of a given situation and how to get the most out of each of them, which opens up the whole field of *motivation theory*;
- *individuals in their roles*: what can be expected of anyone in a particular situation or job and what they expect of others; *role theory* in other words;
- *individuals in groups*: how the individuals can best be combined in groups or teams, what influences their performance and their behaviour in those groups, which is *group theory*.

To put it the other way round: what is your *psychological contract* with the organization? Each of us has an unwritten, unspoken contract with every group or organization to which we belong, be it a class, a school, a club or a family. The contract is psychological, not legal. It balances what you expect to give to that group in return for what you can expect to get. Is it money, or excitement, or achievement, or power or love and security that you want? How much do you want of each, and what will you give in exchange?

Much of the misunderstanding in organizations stems from the fact that the two parties to this unspoken contract have very different ideas of what is in that contract. If you are a teacher you may find that the headteacher thinks that the fact that her or his role is senior to yours and that you are paid a salary entitles her or him to order you to do this or that and to count on your unquestioning obedience and loyalty. To you those might be unreasonable expectations, diminishing to you as an independent individual and as a professional in your own right. Obedience and loyalty you will give, but only where they are earned, where you agree with the aims and purposes and have had your own views and feelings canvassed and taken into account. Both sides can end up seeing the other as unreasonable.

The teacher in turn is 'manager' (see Chapter 1) of a group of children. There is an unspoken set of psychological contracts in every classroom, different no doubt at the front of the class from those at the back. If the teacher's understanding of the contract is not in line with those held by the students, the days will be a continuing series of disappointments, frustrations, anger and disillusion – on both sides.

You cannot be a child in a classroom or a teacher in a school without carrying with you a psychological contract, which is a blend of your view of what motivates you in your role in the group and your estimate of what the other side expects. To be an effective head, therefore, or manager, or, above all, teacher, you need to be aware of what goes into these psychological contracts.

To put it another way, we each have a store of 'E', where it stands for Energy, Excitement, Enthusiasm, Effort, Extra, Especial and so on. We don't distribute that store at random but release it if . . . The 'if' includes speculation that the 'E' will lead to more of something that we value – be that praise, promotion, good marks or popularity. If you, as teacher or as manager, want to bring more of the 'E' out of your charges or your colleagues, you need to know more about what goes on in that (often unconscious) calculation. This does not turn every teacher/manager into an amateur psychologist, because in fact we make guesses about this all the time. We *think* we know what 'motivates' people because we think we know what motivates *us*; so we act on that assumption – and too often get it wrong, because not everyone is like us, particularly when they are not in our job or in our role. Management that is based on the assumption that people are like me is just as likely to be wrong as management on the assumption that everyone else is different from me, greedier, or lazier, or more stupid. We cannot manage, or teach, properly without knowing more about the options, and it is these options that this chapter will explore.

Individuals as individuals

Why do individuals behave as they do? What motivates them? What accounts for their differences? How can they be influenced to do more, better or different? How can they be motivated? There are, broadly, three classes of motivation theory to choose from:

- *Need theories*, which maintain that an individual acts in order to meet a need or set of needs.
- *Goal theories*, which argue that we direct our actions in order to achieve particular goals.
- *Self theories*, which hold that we act to maintain or improve our image of ourselves and therefore our sense of self-respect.

Each set of theories is plausible and explains some of the behaviour we see around us, but none of them explains all of it. Goal theories describe *how* we decide what we do, whereas need and self theories describe *what* goes into that decision.

All of us, we have said, carry around with us *some* theory of motivation, which we apply to those we work with or live with. We may not be conscious of it, let alone know whether it is a 'need theory', a 'goal theory' or a 'self theory', but it will in practice account for a lot of what we do. For instance, if you believe that people are motivated by fear, then you will rationally do everything you can to make them frightened of you. You might well succeed – which would be, to you, just more evidence that you were right. If, on the other hand, you think that the strongest motivator is the chance to achieve something, then you will do your best to put solid achievements within their grasp and to congratulate them when they succeed – once again, but in a different way, giving yourself evidence that you are right. Theories of motivation, in other words, often turn out to be self-fulfilling prophesies, at least in the short term, and so confirm people in particular styles of behaviour that are relatively difficult to change and that can infect the whole group or class with whom they work.

Before you act, therefore, reflect. Or at least be aware of the options available to explain why people do what they do. With this in mind, let us examine the three types of theory.

Need theories

These theories – of which Maslow, Herzberg, McClelland and Alderfer are the main proponents – postulate that people do what they do in order to satisfy certain needs or drives. Once a need is satisfied it no longer motivates; once you are warm, for instance, you won't exert yourself to get warmer. Some put these needs into a hierarchy, suggesting that there are more basic or lower-order needs – physical and economic, for example – which have to be satisfied before the higher-order needs of status and self-fulfilment or achievement come into play. When you feel grossly underpaid, in other words, talk of vocation and the opportunity to change people's lives can fall on deaf ears. That feels true, but there is little hard evidence to support it, except at the extremes. It is more probable that the strength of each need varies with the situation and the occasion (the psychological contract is seldom constant), so that some days we are so tired that all we want is an early night, whilst in early September we are full of enthusiasm for new endeavours and a chance to prove our creativity and competence.

How many needs are there, anyway? One theorist lists thirty. McClelland, a pragmatist in this field, sticks to three: power, achievement and affiliation. He has some evidence to suggest that successful *managers* have high needs for power, moderate needs for achievement and low needs for affiliation. Teachers as a group might be the other way round (we don't know), which could give them difficulties in running a class; they might prefer to be loved than to be respected. McClelland has also demonstrated that you can, through educational experiences, raise people's need to achieve, and that one's early environment has a major effect on which need is stronger. Achievement-minded parents, teachers and class-mates *can* raise one's own need to achieve.

Need theories have done little more than produce a catalogue of possible needs from which you pick according to your pleasure or your cultural environment. The trouble is it is a seductive theory; because the logic says that if you can increase someone's need for something that you can give them, then you can influence, motivate or encourage them to do what you want. 'Motivate' becomes a transitive verb with a subject (you) and an object (them). You have money to offer? Make them greedy. Promotions or prizes? Make them competitive. Sarcasm or sticks? Make them more sensitive.

As individuals, therefore, we want to climb up the layers of needs as quickly as possible to the top layer of personal growth or self-fulfilment because that is where we control our own destinies. As people in control of others we will also, if we are well meaning, increase the opportunities for their self-fulfilment, only to find, of course, that we then lose some of our control over them. It can be frustrating to set pupils or teachers free to do their own thing only to find that they don't then do what you think they ought to do. The temptation is to bring them back into line by reactivating one of their other needs, i.e. by depriving them of something they had taken for granted, such as their standing in the pecking order, your approval or even their annual increment or good report. 'Self-fulfilment is fine for ourselves but risky for others' would be a cynic's comment on Maslow in practice. It leads *some* people to think that the way to motivate others is to keep them *dissatisfied*. Carrots and sticks work only if they like carrots and can't get enough of them, and if they fear sticks.

The easy way to power – and some would say to motivation – is to keep people greedy or *unsatisfied*. Carrots motivate only as long as people can't get enough of them. Need theories can lead to manipulative management. Most teachers are not seduced so easily, but one cannot help wondering what principles of motivation lie behind norm-referenced marking or prizes for only a few. It seems akin to rationing the carrots, and contrasts harshly with the reinforcement theories discussed later on.

Goal theories

Goal theories (sometimes called 'expectancy' or 'path–goal' theory) assume that everyone is at heart rational and that life is a set of calculations of the type 'If I do x will I get y?' The trouble is that each calculation has to start with an assumption that y is desirable, which brings you back to need theory and the relative strength of different y's at different times.

Goal theory, however, has led to some important insights:

- Part of the calculation is your view of the likelihood of getting y if you do x. No matter how desirable y may be, if you don't think you have a chance of getting it then you need not bother trying. Prizes, in other words, or the chance of a headship, matter only to those within spitting distance.
- The x is more critical than the y. y, the end result, can often be quickly agreed in any particular situation. It is the precise steps leading to y that need to be specified; once specified, they become almost goals in themselves. Thus, in setting objectives for managers, the specification of objectives seems to get them moving as much as any promise of reward if they were achieved. In other words, the conditions for success for each individual need to be spelt out. It is not enough just to agree on what success will mean for that person in that situation, although that is a first essential.

● The agreement on x and y between superior and subordinate, teacher and student or parent and child works best when (a) the tasks to be achieved are neither too easy nor too difficult, (b) the superior is seen as a credible source of authority on the connection between x and y and (c) there will be information on progress.

A doctor's recommendation on what to do to avoid another heart attack will often be followed because the above conditions apply. They don't always apply in more day-to-day situations. If the goal is not important to the individual, if they have no respect for the superior, if they know that there is going to be little or no feedback on progress, then the procedure is little more than a polite ritual, exhortation to 'do better in future'.

Goal theories offer an opening for outsiders to become involved in other people's 'E'-type decisions, to open up discussions about 'Why this?' or 'Why me?' They remind one that each teacher and each child makes their own calculation and that nothing about x or y can be taken for granted.

For schools, therefore, goal theories carry some clear messages. Educational objectives should be precise and measurable, and should be measured. Teachers need to be able to say and see where they are getting to; feeling good about the class is not enough. Is it because both goals and feedback are so imprecise in teaching that teachers often find it so depressing when it should be inspiring? Students need first to be sold on the values of the course – if they don't see its value, then no amount of measurable objectives and helpful feedback is going to help. Thereafter they need measurable and achievable *short-term* goals (projects, exercises, etc.), which they see as being relevant to them, and prompt feedback. This is easier said than done, particularly in a class of thirty children with mixed abilities.

Both need and goal theories can be used to explain much short-term behaviour. We can all produce examples of how individuals have changed when a particular need or goal acquires a new importance. The prospect of redundancy or of examinations concentrates the mind wonderfully. In the longer term, however, they seem inadequate answers to the question 'What makes you tick?' This is where self theories come in.

Box 3.1 The performance review

Research in business organizations too often reveals that performance declines as a result of performance reviews or appraisal interviews. How can this be?

Typically the manager starts with a compliment or two and then introduces a few critical comments, either of a general nature or picking up particular incidents over the past year. 'The discipline in your department leaves something to be desired' would be one type of comment. The intention is that the recipient, having similar goals, will accept this as helpful feedback and will reply with remorse and promise to do better.

The comment is however a shock to the subordinate's self-concept, involving a slightly painful readjustment downwards in his or her self-esteem, *if* it is accepted. It is easier, psychologically, *not* to accept the comment but to dismiss it on the grounds (a) that the manager has got the facts wrong, (b) that she or he is incompetent and a bad disciplinarian herself or himself and so need not be heeded or (c) that the job is unimportant anyway, so why take any notice? The net result can therefore be a lower opinion of the boss and the job and a reduced sense of commitment.

To provide critical comment and have it accepted

- the data must be recent and objective, not subjective (so that they cannot be disputed);
- the manager must be credible;
- the manager must demonstrate high regard for the subordinate as a person.

When these conditions do not apply, a performance review can do more harm than good.

These conditions are hard to meet in schools where the criteria for success in teaching are so unclear and where the culture of individualism makes each their own expert. Are schools wise, then, to introduce appraisals? If they practise them properly they are a chance to make goal theory work, with more money (y) paid for meeting agreed objectives (x). But can schools meet the conditions required above?

Self theories

Put simply, we all carry around with us an image of ourselves as we think we are, our *self-concept*, and as we would like to be, our *ego-ideal*. The ego-ideal should be above our self-concept but within reach; if it is too far above we get depressed at our present state, too low and we are too easily satisfied to try harder and can sink into apathy or self-satisfaction. Our sense of self-esteem is healthy when self-concept and ego-ideal are just the right distance apart. High performers, well motivated people, in any field tend to have a good self-concept and an even better ego-ideal. Self-confidence blended with high aspirations seems to be a recipe for good performance.

Our concept of self is formed from many sources. Parents and early life have a lot to do with it. If we see ourselves as incompetent, tentative or stupid it is often because of some childhood experience. The company one keeps, one's peers, are another powerful influence because one tends to see oneself as they are. Lively, active and successful groups feed each other. If you associate with drop-outs you think of yourself as a drop-out. Experience as life goes on all builds one's self-concept. Promotion, praise and recognition enhance it, dismissal and failure push it down again. Essentially, people who feel good perform well.

The message is clear to those who would act on these theories; build up the self-concept, raise expectations and therefore the ego-ideal. Set high standards and build self-confidence. Wherever possible, praise, don't reprimand. If you need to reprimand someone, criticize the act, not the person, so that their self-concept is undamaged. Parents who can scold a child whilst still conveying love know how the trick is done.

The idea of the self-concept is complex. It has generated a lot of study and research and lies at the heart of three subsidiary theories: reinforcement theory, attribution theory, expectancy theory. Studious teachers will have heard of these theories because they have featured more largely in research on schools than in studies of behaviour in other types of organization. They are important, if still imprecise, ways of thinking about people.

Reinforcement theory. In its most general form this theory suggests that reinforcing the individual on every possible occasion enhances the self-concept and self-confidence. There are snags. The person doing the reinforcing has to be credible; praise from someone you despise can even be insulting. Secondly, it has to be clear what you are reinforcing. To praise or reward someone's *effort* may seem to be a slur on their *ability*. I am not necessarily pleased to be complimented on working so hard to change the wheel on the car when I know that someone more skilled than me could have done it in half the time. Thirdly, reinforcement requires patience; it cannot be done until some of the desired behaviour is forthcoming. Fourthly, if applied to the particular behaviour and not to the person, it can look like conditioning or manipulation; remove the reward and the behaviour will stop unless it has gone on long enough to become a habit. Both animals and children have been known to reject their schooling and revert as soon as they are out of the reinforcement environment. *Nevertheless* the general principle of accentuating the positive seems to work better than punishing the negative, because it enhances rather than destroys our self-concept.

Box 3.2 Reinforcement in the classroom

Madsen, Becker and Thomas undertook a carefully planned experiment to introduce positive reinforcement into two primary-school classrooms and monitored the effect on four troublesome children. They first recorded the teacher's 'baseline' or normal behaviour, then observed what happened when the teacher 'ignored' bad or disruptive behaviour as long as it was not physically dangerous, and finally what happened when, in addition to ignoring bad behaviour, the teacher positively rewarded good behaviour. The point of ignoring bad behaviour was the possibility that drawing attention to it actually reinforced and encouraged that bad behaviour.

The results were striking and consistent. The teachers found it difficult to ignore bad behaviour, and when they did so, this was ineffective, on its own, in changing the behaviour of the children. When combined, however, with positive reinforcement the children under study changed markedly and began to smile, co-operate and work constructively.

Cliff showed little change until Mrs A. started praising Appropriate Behaviour, except to get worse during the Ignore phase. He was often doing no academic work, talking to peers, and just fiddling away his time. It took considerable effort by Mrs A. to catch Cliff showing praiseworthy behaviour. As the use of praise continued, Cliff worked harder on his assigned tasks, learned to ignore other children who were misbehaving, and would raise his hand to get teacher's attention. He participated more in class discussions. He was moved up to the fastest arithmetic class.

Reported in C. H. Madsen Jr, W. C. Becker and D. R. Thomas, 'Rules, Praise and Ignoring: Elements of Elementary Classroom Control', *Journal of Applied Behavioral Analysis*, vol. 1, 1968, pp. 139–50.

Attribution theory. This theory is concerned with the way we allocate responsibility for success and failure in ourselves and in others. In general we tend to act to protect or boost our self-concept, by accepting personal responsibility for success but blaming failure on external events or other people. Furthermore, if we have been consistently successful in the past we find it easier both to accept the occasional failure as something outside our control and to believe that other successful people also suffer the occasional misfortune. Consistent failures, on the other hand, are condemned both by themselves and by others, putting even the odd piece of success down to luck or, in some teachers' judgements, cheating. The self-concept in other words is very durable and feeds on itself – once formed it is hard to change, since it finds ways of interpreting the world so as to maintain an image of consistency. Heads and teachers need to be aware of the dangers of stereotyping people and of locking them into a frozen concept of themselves. Sometimes people need to move away altogether in order to escape the labels that they and others have put on themselves.

Expectancy theory. This theory suggests that we can to some extent create self-fulfilling prophecies. If we expect people to perform well, then, indirectly and unconsciously, we shall help them to perform well. The original studies of expectancy theory in *Pygmalion in the Classroom* by Rosenthal and Jacobson have been widely questioned, but there have been sufficient other studies to suggest that, *if* the teacher's higher expectations are shared with and by the student, then performance may well improve. In other words, other people's expectations can alter one's ego-ideal and get one aiming for greater things. But nothing is totally predictable; Hargreaves relates how his *demotion* to a non-O-level class in Latin was such a challenge to his self-concept that he set out to prove the teacher wrong!

All these theories emphasize how important our self-concept is, and our ego-ideal. Self-esteem, said James back in 1890, is a person's success divided by their aspirations. We can bolster our self-esteem by increasing our success or by lowering our aspirations. It is often easier to protect our self-concept from a failure by saying we did not put in enough effort, thereby suggesting that our *ability* was not at fault. Indeed, we may purposefully *not* try hard in order to have an excuse if we fail, thereby ensuring that we do fail. The self-concept is too often self-fulfilling. It is therefore crucial to any understanding of a person's motivation.

Pity the poor teacher then with a classroom, or maybe several class-rooms, of students, each with their own self-concept, which they want to protect. Each has their own sets of needs and goals, each their own *psychological contract* with the teacher and the class – that unspoken unwritten contract which spells out what the individual is prepared to give, by way of effort and commitment, in return for belonging to the group. Pity the poor head with fifty or more teachers, each with their own self-concepts and psychological contracts. No wonder teachers and managers fall back on stereotypes, on simplistic models of motivation, on working on basic needs rather than trying to elevate goals and modify expectations. Organizations, inevitably perhaps, trivialize motivation and personality but in so doing they may put people in boxes for life, prisoners in their views of themselves or dependent on carrots and sticks for any stimulus to do anything. We need to do more to work *with* people rather than *on* them, but the way things are currently organized in schools and other organizations, this can be difficult. Maybe the organization has to change before motivation can improve.

Chapter 2 of *Understanding Organizations* gives a more detailed account of the various theories of motivation, while Chapter 9 of that book discusses how these work out in practice in arrangements for dealing with people in organizations. It is a very important topic but one that is still more to do with one's *beliefs* than with any proven theory. It is interesting that in English we cannot even make up our minds whether 'motivate' is a transitive or intransitive verb!

Individuals in roles

No one can run an organization or a classroom without an understanding of roles and groups. Organizations, after all, are made up of groups of all shapes and sizes, some official and called 'forms', 'departments' or 'committees' and some informal with names like 'clique', 'cabal', 'pressure group' or 'lobby'. Every organization, too, has its sets of roles, some with the formal titles of 'job' or 'responsibility' and others more informal: 'trouble-maker', 'clown', 'leader' or 'helper'.

Both in life and in organizations, however, we make things more difficult than they need be by taking on too many roles at once, by accepting the definitions of our roles without question or by allowing people to make up their own minds about what our roles are meant to be. Similarly we can be tyrannized by groups, letting them get too big, controlling them too loosely, letting particular individuals dominate them or preserving them long after their usefulness has ended. Roles and groups may be inevitable and necessary in organizations, but we do not have to be their passive occupants or victims.

In this section, in the belief that understanding can help to give us more control, we shall examine, briefly:

- the *problems* in roles;
- the *choices* in roles.

The problems in roles

At any one time you are likely to feel the pressures of role ambiguity, role conflict, role overload or even, perhaps, role underload. Any or all of these can distort your life, can result in stress and strain, and can even cause you to fall ill or have a nervous breakdown. Roles are serious things and need to be taken seriously.

Role ambiguity means, obviously enough, that it is unclear what one is meant to do or be in a certain role. That may be because no one has laid down the task or the objective in sufficiently precise terms but merely said, 'Here is the class, get on with it', or 'Try to make the Carol Service into a learning experience' – an invitation rather than an objective. To the strong-minded, this is not ambiguity but freedom, although to the timorous, the new or the shy it can be threatening. More difficult is the ambiguity that results from different people having different expectations of the role. The head may want you, as head of department, to run a syllabus and a teaching strategy devised to produce the maximum of examination success, whilst your staff may have always played down examinations, regarding them as distractions from the true process of learning. It is up to you to resolve the inherited ambiguity in the role, or to live with it.

The most frequently cited causes of role ambiguity are:

- uncertainty about how one's work is evaluated;
- uncertainty about the scope of one's responsibility;
- uncertainty about others' expectations of one's performance;
- uncertainty about the scope for advancement.

One list of the roles of a manager read as follows: Executive, planner, policy-maker, expert, controller of rewards and punishments, arbitrator, exemplar, representative, scapegoat, counsellor, friend, teacher – all aspects of one role, many of them contradictory. All these aspects are part of every *teacher's* job. We saw many of them in the opening vignette of Chapter 1 (Box 1.1). Enriching or overwhelming? It depends on your cast of mind.

Role conflict arises when one of the roles we hold is in conflict with another. Most people have at least two roles, one at work and one at home. Even these can easily get into conflict, with one stealing time and importance from the other. It gets worse if the roles multiply as they tend to do as we get older and more senior, taking on a range of different responsibilities both within and without the workplace. New roles are, of course, exciting and challenging but, if they conflict in time or priorities with existing roles, there can be problems. Chapter 2 explained how role conflict was part and parcel of teaching.

Role overload is one of the problems: just too many responsibilities and not enough hours in the day. That can happen even in one role, if its demands are too great, in other words if the expectations of what can be achieved are too high or if the sheer volume of work is too great. We are usually reluctant to admit that we have reached the limit of our capacities, so that role overload becomes the campaign medal of the busy teacher or administrator. 'I shall not be able to take a proper holiday this year – there is so much to do', and naturally no one else can do it! Role overload is as often self-inflicted as it is imposed on us.

Role underload is the reverse. It is the problem of having a role that does not add up to one's conception of oneself. It is then an insult to one's self-concept, something hard to take lightly. Unemployed people, particularly those made unemployed later in life, are only too well aware of the meaning of role underload, even of role disappearance. In organizations it can lead to cynicism, apathy and destructive behaviour. Many children, particularly those for whom academic work has little appeal, suffer from role underload in school. Given a real task to do, with real responsibility, the new role results in new behaviour.

Role strain. There are positive things to do when these role problems get too big, but those are also our instinctive ways of coping with them when the strain of them gets too much. These coping mechanisms were outlined in Chapter 2, Box 2.3, and consist of:

- *Filtering devices* (to reduce the overload). Do the easy things, not the difficult; sort problems into black or white, no in-betweens; put people, colleagues and pupils into stereotyped boxes; use last year's solutions to this year's problems; do only what *has* to be done, not what ought to be done.
- *Compensation devices* (to relieve the burden). Excessive irritation and emotional outbursts; smoking, drinking or excessive eating; irrational enthusiasms and anger; unconventional friendships or love affairs.
- *Avoidance devices* (to escape the problems). Become difficult to find;

book yourself up with appointments, journeys, meetings and courses; snap at anyone who brings a problem; go home early or arrive late; become ill (genuinely in many cases).

These coping mechanisms alleviate the strain for us but they all hurt the rest of the organization when work is not done properly, colleagues or pupils are abused or neglected and relationships bruised. Many of the personality problems of schools have their source in unresolved role problems, and in the stress that results.

The more positive approach would be to reduce the *ambiguity* by agreeing with everyone what the job is all about (one of the purposes behind job or role descriptions), to reduce the *conflict* by dropping some roles or at least putting clear boundaries around each so that they interfere with each other as little as possible (resolutions to bring no work home in the evenings are an attempt to protect the home role) and to reduce the *overload* by thinking out the priorities properly instead of coping with the crises as they occur. That said, the roles of anyone with any sort of management responsibility remain complex, particularly if she or he is head of a school (see Box 3.3).

Box 3.3 The roles of a manager

Webb and Lyons compared the work done as part of the job of a head-teacher with an analysis of the role of top managers in other organizations. They found remarkable similarities.

- Most managers work at a high intensity of tasks, rapidly dealt with on a face-to-face or telephone basis. 'Their activities are characterized by brevity, variety and discontinuity,' and when they need to undertake a task calling for systematic and reflective consideration of a complex situation, they have to shut themselves away to do it.
- Most managers give higher priority to live rather than delayed needs, and appear to respond to demands for action in preference to abstracted planned work concerned with the future.
- Diary studies have shown that the time span of most of their activities varies between 2 and 20 minutes, with an average between 5 and 10 minutes, that over 70 per cent of these activities involve interacting with other people and that many are of an apparently trivial nature involving only minimal skills – clerical, communicative, technical or ceremonial.
- Small jobs are often carried out by managers when subordinates who could handle them are momentarily not available. This helps them 'to

Box 3.3 – *contd*

keep a line on what is happening'. They prefer talking and listening to reading and give only quick scans to official returns and memoranda to look for triggers for action. They make a lot of use of informal 'soft information' to keep in touch.

From P. C. Webb and G. Lyons, 'The Nature of Managerial Activities in Education', in H. L. Gray (ed.), *The Management of Educational Institutions*, Farmer Press, 1982.

The choices in roles

The other side of the coin to the problems of roles consists of the choices that are available to anyone with responsibility. Rosemary Stewart has pictured a job as in Figure 8. She points out that every job has a list of

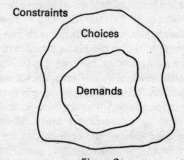

Figure 8

things that have to be done (the *demands*); every job has also a measure of discretion about what is done, when and how (the *choices*). Some jobs clearly have a bigger area of discretion or choice than others, with the job of the headteacher probably having more choice than that of the maintenance man, although many maintenance men *and* heads might dispute that. Every job also has its constraints, most obviously the physical constraints of space, materials, money and people, but also the more intangible constraints of job description, responsibility and accountability. If you want more choice the simplest way is to push back the constraints or to find some way of reducing the strength of the demand (by delegation or automation, for instance).

Stewart's research shows that most managers do not think of themselves as having much choice. Nor do they normally think of negotiating the demands and the contraints. Do teachers? Every individual has probably got more choice than they think they have, and every organization has the power to increase or decrease the discretion or room to choose for the individuals in that organization. A professional organization, as most schools would like to be, will be relatively precise about the demands and constraints on individuals, but will leave wide areas of discretion in between.

Demands include everything that you must do if you are not to fail or lose your job. They include the statutory obligation towards the children in one's care, the institutional requirements of the timetable and the curriculum (if a teacher fails to turn up without good reason, or abandons the agreed syllabus, she or he will have failed to meet the demands of the role). The school can choose to add to those demands by imposing further duties, for out-of-school activities, perhaps, or for committees and study groups, or by requiring particular standards of performance (discipline standards, for instance, or levels of achievement by the pupils), or can leave these to the individual teacher's choice. Similarly a teacher can raise or lower the minimum demands for each pupil.

Constraints start with space, materials and money, but also include the timetable (blocks of time allow more choice than single sessions), and go to the defined responsibilities of each teacher and the others of the school. Is it legitimate, for instance, for teachers to initiate activities and projects outside the classroom? What boundaries does the institution set to individuals' right to innovate? Are noisy classes acceptable or disreputable? The *ground rules* of the organization or the classroom, whether expressed formally or informally, set powerful boundaries to behaviour.

Choices, then, are the room that is left between the demands and the constraints. There is often a choice of *level* of achievement or performance, over and above the minimum level required by the demands of the role. There can be wide choice as to *how* the work is done, particularly in a professional discipline such as teaching. There can even be a choice in the range or *scope* of one's work, again provided the minimum demands are covered. Delegation is one area where the range of choices is wide. Two plant managers, with identical jobs, may split their time very differently:

	Manager A	Manager B
Time with subordinates	70%	40%
Time with boss	6%	6%
Time with other departments	24%	51%
External	—	3%

Manager *A* spends a lot of time supervising his subordinates, helping them and checking their work. Manager *B* is more concerned to see that his subordinates have all the materials, services and support that they require to do their relatively unsupervised work. His job, as he sees it, is to supervise their environment rather than them.

Organizations find it tempting to add to the demands and constraints and to limit choice. That way, you get a more predictable and tidy ship, in which everything runs according to predetermined rules. Teachers find it tempting to run classes in that way. Assembly lines in factories and offices used to be so organized that there was no space at all between demands and constraints, even for talking to your neighbour. Squeeze out choice from a role, however, and you squeeze out individuality, initiative and the room for growth and learning. In the interests of individual and organization it is essential to leave some room for choice. The nature of the task, the abilities of the individual and the acceptable level of risk are factors that need to be considered in reaching a workable compromise.

Worst of all is a situation where the demands and constraints are unspecified, leaving the individual to find out what they are by bumping up against them, by trial and error. Role ambiguity will escalate immediately, initiative will probably decline, and the school will appear to be going in many different directions at once. The findings of Rutter's 15,000-hours study could be reinterpreted as saying that schools where demands, constraints and choices were more clearly marked out seemed to be more effective. That would fit the conclusions of role theory.

Individuals in groups

The problems and opportunities of groups feature in few of the books on leadership and management in schools. At first sight this is strange because schools seem to be made up of groups – classes, year or house groups, departmental or faculty groups, top management groups or 'cabinets', committees, subcommittees and plenty of meetings. Some of them are very odd groups, of course. No manager in her or his right mind would want to work with a group of over 15 individuals let alone 30, which can often be the standard class size. Perhaps, too, the desire of teachers to be seen working with and for individual children makes them want to play down the role of the group, to treat it more as an administrative necessity or burden.

That seems a pity, partly because groups are going to be part of every child's life as they grow up and out into the world, and they might usefully learn to work in and with them (as is now beginning to happen – see Chapter 1). Partly, also, groups *can* be very useful and exciting things, if they are well handled. Why *does* the work group within the classroom seldom survive beyond the primary school and some home economics courses? Why is there so little group teaching, so few group projects by staff and teachers? Is the tradition of individualism in teaching too strong? Is group work considered too expensive? Or is it that the potentialities of the group are not well understood? This section is written in case the last reason is the true one.

The poor image of the group is unfortunate because groups have great advantages for organizations. Consider these facts:

- Groups, surprisingly perhaps, set higher standards for themselves and for the individuals within them than the individuals would on their own. People are spurred on by other people's expectations and are comforted by the collective security of the group, should they fail. Groups may indeed have to be dissuaded from setting unattainable targets for themselves.

- Groups, again perhaps surprisingly, are very kind to their members once the forming and storming stages are over. In the occasional loneliness of an organization the group can provide a psychological home.

- Groups are flexible. It is easier to change the membership of a group, or its purposes, or its standards than it is to change the personnel or structure of the whole organization. Groups can even be discontinued, put on sabbatical or reborn in a way that is not possible with the permanent structures of the school.

- Groups allow individuals to reach beyond themselves, to be part of something that none of them could have attained on their own and to discover ways of working with others to mutual benefit. Groups, in other words, are more than the sum of their parts.

Groups, of course, can live up to their stereotype. They can be ineffective, boring, harmful and destructive. They can make a camel instead of a horse. Because they are powerful organizational tools they can be turned against the organization and the individual. They need to be handled properly; they can be, but it does not happen by chance. This section explains some of the factors that make effective groups. We do not have to be the victims of groups. We have choices over the purposes of these groups, their size, their process and the roles of their participants.

The purposes of groups

Purpose is the first area of choice. Groups have many possible purposes, which unfortunately can overlap, get in each other's way, conflict or confuse. The spectrum of possible purposes is wide. Organizations use groups, committees or meetings for the following purposes:

- To take decisions (about the range of subject choices).
- To share out the work (in a department).
- To oversee the work (the governors).
- To solve problems (a task force).
- To collect and share information (a departmental meeting).
- To test and ratify decisions (an examinations board).
- To co-ordinate and liaise (heads of house meeting).
- To increase involvement and commitment (start-of-year get-to-gether).
- To negotiate and resolve conflicts (a negotiating team).
- To investigate the past (a commission of inquiry).

Individuals use groups:

- To share in a common activity.
- To promote a cause or an idea.
- To gain status or power.
- To have friends and 'belong'.
- Because it is part of their job.

Ideally, one needs different groups for different purposes, even if many of the members of those groups are the same. To collect or share information, for instance, would suggest as large a group as possible, while a problem-solving group should not exceed 6 or 7 members if everyone is going to have a chance to contribute. If you want to distribute status as widely as possible, it would be sensible to make your group very large, like the 'partnerships' of professional firms, but then the group is too large for decision-making or problem-solving. So be it, a further inner group has to be formed for that purpose, with big decisions tested out and ratified by the larger group.

It can be a dangerous economy to try to do everything with just one group, to create one small all-purpose 'cabinet' at the top of the school. Such a group might be good for some of the purposes but it may be too small for the proper collection and sharing of information, may have the wrong people for solving some problems and will inevitably reduce the commitment of those who are excluded. It is better, in the long run, to have a number of groups with different purposes but overlapping membership, or at least to have different meetings of the same group for different purposes.

The choice of purpose will, after all, affect the people who are needed in the group, the size of the group, how the meeting or the work is to be organized, how or if decisions are to be taken, whether a leader is needed and if so what his or her function is. *First choose your purpose, then choose your group.* That, of course, is not always possible. Groups are often there whether you like them or not. There is an ex-officio membership of some formal groups, while other, more informal groups come into being just because people are next to each other (proximity), like each other (affinity) or have similar interests (communality). These are the groups that many a head or teacher would rather not have; but again the message must be, if you find yourself with a group, try to influence its purpose. A clique of friends can easily turn into a group in search of a purpose, and the purpose that comes to hand is not always going to be to the liking of the institution. The instinctive reaction of those in control of the institution is to break up the group, which may only have the effect of driving it underground. A more positive approach would be to recognize the reality of the group and to help it choose a purpose and a task more in tune with the school's ideas.

The size of groups

Size is the second opportunity for choice. There is no one best size, because that depends on the purpose, but there are two contradictory forces that always apply:

- *the larger* the group the greater the number of people who can listen, learn and contribute their knowledge or experience;
- *the smaller* the group the more chance there is for each individual to contribute, to get to know the others and to feel committed to the working of the group and to its products or conclusions.

Every group therefore tends to be a compromise between getting it small enough to work (usually thought to be between 3 and 9 members) and big enough to be comprehensive. Double-figure groups become less effective as working groups as they grow until they become sensible to use only for disseminating information, testing and ratifying decisions or reporting. Full staff meetings cannot be problem-solving occasions except in a primary school. A class of thirty pupils constitutes a group useful only for disseminating information or reporting results; any problem-solving has to be done by individuals working alone or in small sub-groups. Group theory would suggest that a class of 30 was an inefficient compromise between classes of 50 or 60 for lectures and groups of 7 for problem-solving.

Small, however, is not always beautiful. Small, cohesive and all-purpose groups at the top of institutions have, on too many occasions, produced the phenomenon known as 'group think'. 'Group think' happens when a comfortable and cohesive group let their desire for consensus override their good sense when looking at all the options for the future. They end up by choosing a compatible rather than the best plan. Janis, who invented the term, has described the symptoms:

- The members discuss only a few solutions and ignore other alternatives.
- They fail to examine the adverse consequences of their preferred solution.
- They too quickly drop alternatives that at first appear unsatisfactory.
- They make little effort to get the advice of specialists.
- They fail to work out contingency plans for failure.

Too many organizations, including schools, are run by a closed oligarchy. With the best of intentions these oligarchies can lead the institution down the road of the comfortable rather than the best. Janis quotes the Bay of Pigs fiasco as an example of a 'group think' blunder, followed by the successful outcome to the Cuban missile crisis when President Kennedy had learnt, painfully, that he needed to open up his decision-making clan.

The process of groups

The process or the 'dynamics' of the group offers a third possibility of choice. Groups, like individuals, appear to have a clearly defined growth cycle, which has been described in four stages:

- *Forming* – an edgy process of sniffing each other out, in which each individual eventually makes his or her mark and displays a little of their agenda.
- *Storming* – a period of conflict, sometimes about the aims of the group, sometimes about the aims of individuals, in which the first easy but false consensus is challenged.

- *Norming* – a resettling into an acceptable way of working, with goals and roles more understood and accepted.
- *Performing* – a mature and a sensibly productive phase, which allows argument and discussion but within an agreed set of objectives.

Groups seem to need their period of adolescence, and it is folly to try to prevent or to contain this. Groups who have not gone through these stages are false groups, meeting to observe a ritual but not likely to produce anything significant. Constant changes of membership, new leaders or too short meetings will get in the way of this cycle of growth. Long meetings in the early days of a group will often help the group to grow even if they are at times traumatic.

The process by which groups reach *decisions* is not inevitable, however. The group can choose to go for

- decision by the leader;
- decision by majority;
- decision by consensus;
- decision by minority;
- decision by no response.

The last two happen by mistake. Ideas are dropped because no one says anything (no response) or because a few feel deeply opposed (minority). Good ideas can disappear down these plug-holes if the group does not make a more determined choice of procedure. Which decision-making process is chosen will largely depend on the purpose of the particular group. If its purpose is to advise the head, then the head will *take* the decision even if the group helps him or her to *make* it. Large groups, which often have a representative element in their membership, tend to fall back on majority voting if they cannot reach consensus. The clever leader is anxious to avoid imposing her or his decision and will therefore strive to sense any emerging consensus so that the members of the group feel that they have some ownership of the final outcome.

The *procedure* of the meeting is another area of choice. The chairman can run the group like a wheel, with the chair at the hub, as it were, and individuals reporting and speaking to the hub. Alternatively it can be a more or less leaderless group with everyone interacting with everyone, an all-channel group. Research and experience show that the more directed wheel form is quicker although the quality of the work is heavily influenced by the quality of the chairman or leader. The all-channel free-form group is better at more complicated problems and is more satisfying to its members, but does take longer. Under pressure of time this form of group will often reform itself into a wheel, in order to get things finished. The answer seems to be horses for courses, as in most organizational matters; where the problem is vague or complex (often in the initial stages) the all-channel format is desirable, but when the work separates out into different aspects or tools, the wheel is preferable. Heads of school or department, however, who in the interest of time and efficiency run all groups as a wheel are running the risk of losing some of the potential creativity in the group.

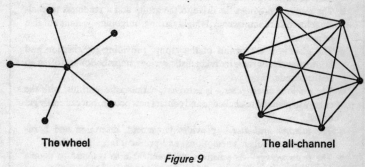

The wheel   **The all-channel**

Figure 9

The setting and the seating for the group are often the outward and visible signs of the procedure to be followed. A formal setting, perhaps round a sort of board-table, will indicate a wheel format; easy-chairs in a circle suggest an all-channel procedure. If a group is to change its style midway through a meeting it is often sensible to make some change to the setting so that group members get a clear message as to what type of meeting each part is intended to be. Signals influence behaviour.

The roles in a group

Nowhere is the language of roles more obvious than in a group. We all play a variety of roles in any group, whether it be a departmental meeting, a class or a sports team. Groups, as we shall see, need a mix of roles and types of people if they are to perform well, but it cannot be just any old mix. Anyone who wants to get the best out of their group needs to ponder and if possible influence the mix.

Box 3.4 Belbin's balance

Based on research at Henley Management College and in industry, Dr Meredith Belbin has been able to describe the kind of mix of personalities that a productive team should have. There are eight of them.

- *The company worker* – has organizing ability, is hard-working and self-disciplining. He or she is conservative, predictable and dutiful and can lack flexibility.
- *The chairman* – is calm, self-confident and controlled, with a strong sense of objectives, unprejudiced and not necessarily particularly clever.
- *The shaper* – provides the drive to the group and a readiness to challenge inertia or complacency, is highly strung, outgoing, dynamic but also impatient.
- *The plant* – is the genius of the group, providing imagination and knowledge. He or she is individualistic, serious, unorthodox and often up in the clouds.
- *The resource investigator* – is extrovert, enthusiastic, curious, with the energy to respond to challenge and contact new people, but can easily get bored.
- *The monitor–evaluator* – provides judgement, discretion and hard-headedness, is sober, unemotional and prudent, but can be dull.
- *The team worker* – is sensitive, mild and able to respond to people and promote the team spirit, although he or she can be indecisive in crises.
- *The complete finisher* – is the perfectionist, painstaking, conscientious and orderly, as well as having a tendency to worry about small things.

Belbin believes that most people have a preferred role but also a back-up one. The balanced group really needs all eight.

R. Meredith Belbin, *Management Teams: Why They Succeed or Fail*, Heinemann, 1981.

Box 3.4 lists eight roles that are needed in an effective team. Simpler models bring it down to three:

- the logical thinker;
- the strong fighter;
- the friend and helper.

An even simpler vision requires that there be someone who is concerned about the *task* – that it should be pushed forward, be of the required standard and be completed – while someone else is concerned with the *process* of the group.

The point is that a cosy group of like-minded friends (e.g. the English Dept?) may be very comfortable but may not get the work done as well as a more mixed group of talents and personalities. But how do you get this mixed bag to pull together? 'With difficulty' is the short answer, but it helps if there is a common objective that all believe in, and mutual respect. There may not at first sight be much that the leader can do about mutual respect if it does not exist to begin with; but as Belbin's list in Box 3.4 reveals, there is a wide range of personalities that can be useful in a group, and a wise leader will make sure that the useful parts of an individual's character are pulled into the service of the group. The common objective is, however, crucial. Without a shared ambition for the group each member will be tempted to use the group to further their personal goals, whatever they may be. In time of national emergency we sink our political differences; so it is in groups. Routine, ritualistic standing committees, made up of representatives and office-holders, are the most difficult to turn into effective *teams*, because they seldom have any uplifting, inspiring or overriding goals. If ever the opportunity arises to turn such a group into a project team or an emergency war cabinet, the morale will often improve dramatically and the work of the group move into a new gear. The argument has gone full circle; *purpose is paramount* in handling groups.

There is more, much more, that could be said about the understanding of individuals – as themselves, in their roles or in their groups. Some of that can be found in the companion volume, *Understanding Organizations*, together with more examples and with references to other works. It is a huge topic. So it should be, and since they are to most children the first formal organization they have ever known, schools are actually the most powerful organization model in our society. It is important, very important, that they get it right.

David Hargreaves has argued that the belief in and the cultivation of *individualism* has gone too far in secondary schools in Britain, so far that it seems more like the encouragement of egoism, or the selfish pursuit of one's own interest. He argues for 'dignity' as a central aim in education, defining this as a 'sense of being worthy, of possessing creative, inventive and critical capacities, of having the power to achieve personal and social change'. He goes on to point out that this dignity depends, first, on the person acquiring competences and a sense of making a valid contribution to the life of the group to which she or he belongs, and secondly on the person having a sense of being valued by others in those groups. Groups, in other words, are essential to Hargreaves's view of education. The individual cannot exist for long or for good without roles and groups. How odd, then, that these should have been so little recognized in the talk of schools and classrooms; how encouraging, on the other hand, to find the ideas of active group learning springing up on the pastoral side of the secondary school.

4 Running the Organization

Important as it is to understand the individuals in a school, be they teachers or pupils, and their relationship to their roles and to each other, this cannot be the end of the matter. People behave as they do to a large extent because they are told to do so, because they are expected to or because they believe that someone else knows best. Organizations work, in other words, because there are rules and regulations, systems of authority, people who know best and traditions as to 'how things should be done around here'. It is naïve to think that a school could be run like Alcoholics Anonymous, where everyone in the group has the same aim and voluntarily accepts a code of discipline and behaviour. Where, then, should power reside in a school and how should it be distributed? Are the political games and schemings that go on in all organizations a bad thing, or just inevitable? What kind of organization should a school be? *Should* it be the autocracy that many schools are thought to be, a private fiefdom of the head; or, at the other extreme, should it be more like a professional group enjoying the licensed anarchy of a collective of individuals? Are there any other options?

As in all aspects of organizations, there is no one right answer. So much, as we shall see, depends on what you believe are the priorities for the organization or, indeed, on what you think is the 'proper' way of running things. Schools, however, can be prisoners of their culture, so locked into their own world that they become afflicted by their own variety of 'group think', unaware that there are more ways than they know of to run their organization. This does not mean that schools need to ape businesses, universities or even co-operatives, but they do need to *understand* what different cultures, structures and systems of control are open to them, and what the advantages and disadvantages are of each.

There are fuller discussions of these possibilities in Chapters 5, 7 and 8 of the companion book, *Understanding Organizations*, and some account of what they mean in practice in Chapters 10 and 11. In this chapter we shall take a brief look at:

● the systems of *power* and *control* that are worth considering;

- the alternative models of an organization, and their implications, that a school can choose from;
- the choices of structure and what determines them.

The systems of power and control

'Power' is an unpopular word. It has feudal overtones, suggesting that one person can be another's slave or serf. It sits ill with modern concepts of the rights of the individual and with a teacher's assumptions of professional autonomy. It is also semantically confusing. It does not have a verbal form of its own, for instance, so that when we want to talk about exercising power we start to use verbs like 'influence' or 'control'. There is therefore a whole literature about the differences between power and influence, authority and control. The ordinary person, however, seems to know quite well what is meant. When, as part of a research project by Selancik and Pfeffer, ten department managers in an insurance company were asked to rank twenty-one of their colleagues by their degree of influence in the organization, only one of the ten bothered to ask what 'influence' meant. He was told 'power', said 'oh' and got straight on with the task. The ten ranked their colleagues in remarkably similar ways.

In this book, 'power' has the more general meaning of the ability to affect a situation. For all practical purposes 'influence' means the same as 'power', with the added advantage that it is also a verb. When power, or influence, is legitimate, recognized and acknowledged it is called 'authority'. A terrorist, therefore, has power but not authority; a troublesome pupil too can have power without authority, whilst the teacher has authority. That does not however necessarily make things easier!

You can get power in various ways:

- By control of resources, money, guns, information or brute physical strength. 'How many tanks has the Pope?' said Stalin, suggesting that only *resource power* counted. He was wrong.
- By occupying a position or formal role in an institution or in society. This *position power* becomes authority because your power is then licensed. The position power will ultimately turn out to be backed up by resource power; the police would have little authority without the law courts behind them, which is why any police force will, from time to time, want to increase the severity of the sentences or its own resource power (e.g. guns).

- By possessing knowledge, expertise or wisdom, which gives one *expert power*. This, if widely accepted, gets turned into authority of another sort, as when we say of someone, 'He or she is an authority on . . .'. This kind of authority is, however, not backed up by resource power and therefore has to be self-enforcing. If you refuse to believe anything you read in this book, we can do nothing about it!
- By possessing some kind of charisma, which may come from your personality, from your association with other great people (what is called 'referent power') or from your track record – *personal power*.

There are two things to notice about these sources of power:

First, resource power and position power, the first two, are usually given to you from above, or from outside, in organizations. The head-teacher is given a degree of discretion over money, promotions, appointments and sundry other 'goodies'. She or he, by virtue of the role, is able to tell a lot of people to do things, to exercise authority. Expert power and personal power, on the other hand, are given to you from underneath, from the very people over whom you will sometimes exercise that power. You can *claim* to be an expert or a great character, but if no one believes you it remains an empty claim. Expert power and personal power are therefore the most acceptable types of power in schools because they need no enforcing, they carry their own authority and they are welcomed by the people to whom they are applied.

Secondly, depending on what type of power you think you have, you can or cannot do various things. Resource power and position power allow you to lay down rules and regulations, issue orders and instructions, take decisions about other people and, generally, be a 'boss'. You don't *have* to do all these things, of course, but you *can*. But they are not necessarily going to happen unless you check – that is, if these are your only sources of power – which is why large and impersonal organizations usually have to accompany their authority with control systems of various types. Resource power and position power, *on their own*, are not self-enforcing. If your staff or your pupils do not respect you, or respect the school as a whole, you will have to spend more of your time than you would like checking up on them. In the jargon of the subject, resource power and position power are responded to with *compliance*. Expert power and personal power, by contrast, allow you to influence people by persuasion and example. People do as you ask, not because of possible punishment or because of your title, but because they respect you, understand and agree with you, or because they believe in what you are trying to do even if they don't understand it. They respond with *identification*, which, if it is strong enough, needs no checking. Better still, they *internalize* your wishes, making them part of themselves.

The sources of power are not mutually exclusive. You can have them all at the same time. Indeed, every head and every teacher would like to think that they never need to use their resource or position power, that their own personal reputation and credibility are enough and that reason and persuasion will be sufficient in a rational world. It would be nice if it were so, but even in a family it does not always work out like that, let alone in a large school. Any parent who has had to say, 'Because *I* say so', or 'No television for you tonight', will know that position and resource power are useful and necessary things to have up one's sleeve. Just because you have *authority* you cannot expect everyone to *agree* with you even if they *obey* you. It is important to remember these things when we are in positions of power and influence, lest we kid ourselves.

Box 4.1 Where does authority come from?

Basis of authority	A police department	A welfare office	A school
Legal	27%	43%	35%
Position	66%	95%	60%
Competence	15%	22%	45%
Personal	42%	13%	15%

The figures add up to more than 100 per cent because most participants in the research mentioned more than one source of authority. The school reflects the professional tradition, with a high weighting given to competence, whereas the welfare office is seen as heavily bureaucratic (position power) and the police as a mix between officialdom and personality.

Based on research in these organizations by Peabody, reported in 'Perceptions of Organizational Authority', *Administrative Science Quarterly*, 1962.

It is sensible therefore to be aware of the possible power or influence systems that can be found in any organization and are sure to be in every school. The choice is not of one rather than the others, but of the nature of the mix. Which ones would you like to predominate, and how do you do it?

Mintzberg has usefully identified four types of system of influence and control at work:

- the system of authority;
- the system of ideology;
- the system of expertise;
- the system of politics.

We need to say a few words about each before drawing any conclusions.

The system of authority

In any large formal organization the head needs to control the behaviour of the people to whom she or he has delegated formal power and the people to whom they have delegated and so on down the line. She or he will therefore give work orders, set the parameters of decisions, review decisions and allocate resources. This is their *personal control system*. They will also produce or have produced a set of rules and regulations, standing orders, job descriptions, reporting mechanisms, plans and objectives. This is their *bureaucratic control system*. All formal organizations need these two systems; and, as we saw in Chapter 3, specific objectives, constraints and standards are necessary for motivation.

These two control systems stem from position power backed by resource power. It is the legitimate right, and the duty, of anyone in a position of responsibility to set up these systems. The details can and should be discussed, so that they are as appropriate and as cost-effective in time and money as possible, but it is the position-holder's task to set them going.

Any head or teacher, however, who felt that these were all that were necessary to hold the school or the class together would be mistaken.

The system of ideology

This system is more intangible, but no less important for that. It seeks to build up the feeling of 'membership' of the organization, to help people identify with the traditions and the mission of the place, so that they will all pull together and sink their differences in pursuit of a common enemy. The armed forces, for example, rely heavily on a system of ideology that they would call 'loyalty', but other organizations also seek to build up an identification with the organization and a commitment to its traditions and mission. They use a process known as *socialization*, in which new recruits learn the ways of the place from official literature and from the example of key models, from myths and stories of the past. Symbols and rituals are important in maintaining a system of ideology; dinners, ties, badges and clubs are all used by organizations.

It may sound Machiavellian but it makes sense, for the individual as well as for the organization, to build up the image of the institution. Individuals, as we suggested in Chapter 3, gain their dignity and their sense of worth from their contributions to, and acceptance by, a group. They want to feel that the group is worth contributing to and not to feel demeaned by wearing its emblems or attending its functions. The cult of individualism suggests that in some way you sacrifice your autonomy if you so obviously 'belong', yet if the 'belonging' is to something valued it does not feel like a sacrifice.

For the comprehensive school the system of ideology has often been a dilemma. The symbols and rituals traditional to schools – uniforms, prizes, distinctions, school teams and school songs – have seemed inappropriate to their proclaimed ideology of equality. The old symbols and rituals have therefore been abandoned by many schools, but they have not always been replaced, leaving equality to be symbolized by a sort of nothingness. That is unfortunate, even if understandable, because we know from a range of other institutions that if you believe in the institution, are proud to be there and have a way of expressing that commitment and pride you will perform better. The army regiments, the big successful charities, the Japanese business corporations, the champion football teams all demonstrate this; ideology, with its accompanying symbols and rituals, is a powerful system of influence. Schools may have too readily thrown the baby out with the bathwater of unwanted symbolism.

But the system of ideology must have more to it than rituals and symbols. People are not idiots. They need to know what it is they are being asked to identify with before they buy the process. The system has to hang from a vision, from a sense of mission that provides the *raison d'être* of the institution. At its heart the system of ideology is saying that nothing binds people together more, or is more compelling, than belief in a common cause, as we noted in the case of groups. It is however too easy and too rash to assume that the mission is understood and the vision shared by all. Successful leaders go to great lengths to articulate the mission and to act out their beliefs in their own lives. Schools, just like other organizations, are full of people with very different reasons for being there. Some are there because they have to be, some for the money, some for the friends, and some because they want to learn or to teach. To bind these very different groups together needs inspiring ideals, inspiring examples and inspiring words. To create and maintain a system of ideology is not easy, nor quick.

The ideology will have at its heart a philosophy of education, a clear understanding of what people are being educated in and for – what the school stands for, in other words – as well as a consistent approach to *how* that education is to be done and the sort of standards that are to be looked for. This philosophy needs then to be articulated, not just in the formal prose of the school's prospectus, but in the everyday utterances and behaviour of its members. An ideology needs its outward and visible signs; only then does it begin to be the uniting system of influence that it should be.

The system of expertise

Complex organizations, however, have to go beyond the systems of authority and ideology. There is no way that you can control what goes on in every individual classroom or in all the operating theatres of a hospital by direct supervision or by rules and regulations. There are too many unpredictables. These organizations have to rely on their professionals and their guaranteed expertise. The level of expertise of any professional is such that they have to be largely trained and certified *outside* the organization. That done, they can be assumed to possess standardized skills so that the organization can be planned and controlled on the assumption that a surgeon, any surgeon, can do certain operations, assisted by an anaesthetist, any anaesthetist. In fact the two do not actually have to speak, or even to know each other, in order to work together on a successful operation.

A school, therefore, should be able to organize itself around a complement of professional teachers at the required levels in the required subjects or disciplines and then let them loose to do their own professional thing. If the skills of teaching could be standardized enough, taught well enough, properly certificated and continually validated, the system of expertise would be an adequate and self-controlling system for keeping the place going.

Things are not quite that standardized, however, nor does all the work of the school happen in the classrooms. Every school needs more than the system of expertise even if 'professionalization' was extended to include the cleaners and the maintenance people as well as the teaching staff. Nevertheless the traditions of professionalism run deep and strong. There are many teachers who cannot really see why any other system than that of expertise is needed to run a school, and who therefore find the bureaucracy and conformity required by the other systems an insult to their profession and evidence of a reluctance to give up power by those at the top.

They are right in a way. The system of expertise is not a comfortable one for anyone sitting in the centre trying to hold the thing together. There are few strings to pull. The only real control is over recruitment. As one head said, 'If I want to change this place I can only do it by appointing some new heads of department and then waiting for five years.'

It is even more complicated than that. Power in the system of expertise goes to those professionals in control of 'critical functions'. If the fame or fortune of an institution happens to rest on the standard of its science teaching, then the head of science is extremely powerful. But it might be sport, or music, or even the appearance of the grounds. That is fair enough unless you happen, as head, to want to change the priorities of the school or even to modify the science or music curriculum. Under a fully fledged professional system of expertise you will not get very far. Systems of expertise, in short, work well where tasks do not have to be linked together, where each can do their own thing without affecting anyone else or the institution. Medical practices, firms of solicitors, barristers in chambers – where each have their own clients – can thrive with only a system of expertise to hold them together. It is more difficult in a school.

The system of politics

It is politics with a small 'p', and it is less a system than a proliferation of ways in which those inside the institution fight back against the other systems of influence. The insiders need to exert influence too and will never put too much reliance on any formal methods of consultation or participation. Organizational politics are correctly seen as disruptive, inconvenient and a problem by those who are trying to run the place, but they are the inevitable result of having autonomous individuals and of giving them discretion. They will naturally want to exert influence upwards and sideways as well as downwards. The trouble is that none of the other three systems works *upwards* (except in one or two cases of specialist expertise); therefore the insiders have to find other ways, and they do.

The most obvious way to subvert the official influence systems is to distort the objectives for one's group. In factories the work groups would often fix the rate of output below their capacity in order to make life easier for themselves. Service departments, required to reduce costs, can most easily do it by reducing the service; a librarian might for instance cut the library costs by closing the library at lunch-time. Other groups, in order to boost their own importance or keep themselves busy, will sometimes ensure that others remain dependent on them; maintenance teams may keep equipment under-serviced so that they become more important and therefore more powerful; remedial teachers want backward children and can, consciously or unconsciously, slow their progress to boost their empire.

These devices can be picked up and corrected by the formal authority system if it is working correctly. But there are other ways in which insiders seek to influence the institution, either for its own good or for theirs. Mintzberg (in Box 4.2) lists thirteen games people play in organizations, taking advantage of the fact that even the lowliest has the power to stop something if not to start it. In the end, that is, the school's work depends on someone lighting the boiler at the right time – someone who therefore has the power, if she or he wants to use it, to frustrate the organization.

This form of *negative power*, therefore, is available to anyone who wants to use it to further their own ends. It is no surprise to find that trade unions, in all organizations, are adept at exploiting it in order to inconvenience and, indeed, to threaten the organization. The only way to counter this power, apart from dealing with it in a bargaining mode, is to build up the system of ideology, on the grounds that people will seldom want to attack something they believe in. Teachers on strike will, as decent professionals committed to the school and its children, find themselves pulled one way by the ideology and another way by the need to use political negative power to advance their own cause.

The system of politics is less active and less potent in small organizations because it is easier to get a shared ideology in a small place and to deal with an individual's worries, grouses and complaints. Small organizations are, therefore, more likely to be friendly co-operative places with fewer 'games' going on and more of a common feeling. It is not guaranteed to be that way, of course, for small can be ugly, imprisoning and bitchy (as many families will testify), but it should be easier if not more beautiful.

If the system of politics is highly visible and active it is a sure sign that the system of authority and the system of ideology are not working as well as they might be. In that case the political system may be the trigger for change, but it will divert energy and distract attention from the main problems and will lower morale in the school. A gently rumbling system of politics, however, may be no bad thing – a useful corrective to the autocratic or oligarchic tendencies in every school. Sensible headteachers don't worry too much about most of the games, but alarm bells should ring if the last three in Box 4.2 look like beginning.

Box 4.2 Organizational games

Games to resist authority:	● The Insurgency Game (overt or covert disobedience using negative or blocking power).
Games to counter resistance:	● The Counter-insurgency Game (sudden inspections, overlapping responsibilities, competing groups).
Games to build power bases:	● The Sponsorship Game (find a sponsor from your superiors).
	● The Alliance Game (with colleagues).
	● The Empire-Building Game (with subordinates).
	● The Budgeting Game (bid for more resources than you need).
	● The Expertise Game (hoard your knowledge).
	● The Lording Game (play the rules by the letter to exaggerate your importance to colleagues or clients).
Games to defeat rivals:	● The Line versus Staff Game (operators against advisers).
	● The Rival Camps Game (between factions or departments).
Games to change the organization:	● The Strategic Candidates Game (building support for a particular protagonist).
	● The Whistle-Blowing Game (blowing the gaff on an issue to an influential outsider).
	● The Young Turks Game (a *coup d'état* by a group against the leader).

From H. Mintzberg, *Power In and Around Organizations*, Prentice-Hall, 1983, pp. 188–217.

Nobody can run a class or a school without some sort of power base and some system of influence and control. Most people will use a mix of all four systems and all four sources of power, but life would have fewer surprises if we knew which one we were relying on at any given time.

What this analysis demonstrates is that it is not enough to have a set of school rules and a fine staff; you also need a vision and a sense of mission to bond everyone together and must tolerate the kind of modging and negotiating that is the stuff of organization politics. One recent view of leadership, by MacGregor Burns, distinguishes between *transactional leadership* (getting things done) and *transforming leadership* (pointing the way or inspiring) and argues that the best leaders combine both. Easy to say, difficult to do, whether in class or in school, but one without the other is not enough.

The choice of cultures and models

Every organization is different. Each school is different from every other school; and schools, as a group, are different from other kinds of organization. There is something natural and right about that, for organizations are living things, each with its own history and traditions and environment and its own ability to shape its destiny. It would be a very dull and uncreative world if there was only one way to design and run an organization, just as it would be a dull and uncreative world if all families were exactly the same. Nevertheless there are things that are true of all families, and, in spite of their differences, there are some truths and theories that apply to all organizations, be they schools or hospitals or banks.

It was a recognition of the essential rightness of differences that led to the development of the idea of organizational cultures. A culture, according to the Chambers Dictionary, is the 'total of the inherited ideas, beliefs, values and knowledge, which constitute the shared bases of social action' and 'the total range of ideas and activities of a group of people with shared traditions which are transmitted and reinforced by members of a group'. The French culture is different from the English one although physically only twenty miles of water separate the two peoples. In the same way, a bank is a different culture from an oil refinery, and a hospital works on cultural assumptions different from those of an insurance company or of a school.

In some organizations, and some schools, everything is tight and tidy and precise. People wear uniforms, things run to precise timetables, individuals are addressed formally by their title ('Headmistress') or by their surname ('Mrs Pierce'); there are rules and procedures for everything, and things are expected to go 'by the book'. In other places life seems much more informal, less structured and less regulated. 'Bill' or

'Mary' gets on with their own work; results are everything – provided they are good no one seems to worry too much about how they are achieved. In some organizations there are clearly bosses and workers, in others the leadership seems more diffused, people can have three or even four superiors and can even work in a group led by one of their subordinates. In one place everything will be hurry and bustle, in another calm and precision. The things prized in one organization (music, or good sports results, say) will be discounted in another. Some organizations will boast that people never leave them, others thrive on a constant change of personnel. Do you speak your mind or keep your mouth shut; work as hard as you can or as little as you can? Are you motivated by the work itself, or by the security of belonging to a good institution? Do you feel that you have 'bosses' or only 'colleagues'? It all depends on the culture of the organization.

A fourfold classification of cultures or 'ideologies' was first outlined by Dr Roger Harrison, although earlier organization theorists had developed two-sided models (e.g. organic and mechanistic, or calculative and coercive). This was developed by Handy into a more comprehensive description of four cultural types, with indications of when and where each culture might be expected to thrive and how the four types blend together to form each individual organization's cultural mix. This is described and explained in Chapter 7 of *Understanding Organizations*.

The work on cultures had, however, been largely based on business organizations and public corporations. Would it have any relevance for school organizations? An exploratory study by Handy, which included opportunities to complete a questionnaire on the perceived culture of the school, suggests that all four cultures *can* be observed in schools, that each school has its own mix, and that the cultural dilemmas that affect other organizations are there in the schools as well. This does not mean that schools will necessarily find the same way out of those dilemmas that other organizations do. It means only that one way of looking at organizations can be used to understand some of the dilemmas of schools as organizations. Understanding is not enough, of course. It does not automatically help you to know what to do, but it is the first step towards sensible action. If one grows up in one system, one culture, knowing only that culture, then it is not always evident that there are alternative ways to do things. The cultural traditions of the professions are sometimes so strong that their organizations (be they schools, hospitals, law courts or universities) seem to have grown up in different countries from the many other organizations all around them. They have invented their own organizational models, unaware that there was a range of models to choose from.

The four cultures are:

- The club culture.
- The role culture.
- The task culture.
- The person culture.

It must be emphasized at the beginning that there are no wholly good cultures and no wholly bad cultures. All cultures are good in the right place, because each culture is good for some things and less good for others.

The club culture

The best picture to describe this kind of organization is a spider's web, because the key to the whole organization sits in the centre, surrounded by ever-widening circles of intimates and influence. The closer you are to the spider the more influence you have. There are other lines in the web – the lines of responsibility, the functions of the organization – but the intimacy lines are the important ones, for this organization works like a club, a club built around its head.

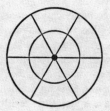

Figure 10

The 'organizational idea' in the club culture is that the organization is there to extend the person of the head or, often, of the founder. If she or he could do everything themselves, they would. It is because they can't that there has to be an organization at all; therefore the organization should be an extension of themselves, acting on behalf of them, a club of like-minded people. That can sound like a dictatorship, and some club cultures are dictatorships of the owner or the founder, but at their best they are based on trust and communicate by a sort of telepathy with everyone knowing each other's mind. They are very *personal* cultures, for the spider preserves his or her freedom of manoeuvre by writing little down, preferring to talk to people, to sense their reactions and to infect them with her or his own enthusiasms or passions. If there are memoranda, or minutes of meetings, they go from 'Simon' to 'Christine', or more often from set of initials to set of initials, rather than from job title to job title.

Club cultures therefore are rich in personality. They abound with almost mythical stories and folklore from the past and can be very exciting places to work *if* you belong to the club and share the values and beliefs of the spider. Their great strength is in their ability to respond immediately and intuitively to opportunities or crises because of the very short lines of communication and because of the centralization of power. Their danger lies in the dominance of the character of the central figure. Without a spider the web is dead. If the spider is weak, corrupt or inept, or picks the wrong people, the organization is also weak, corrupt, inept or badly staffed.

These cultures thrive where personality and speed of response are critical, in new business situations, in deals and brokerage transactions, in the artistic and theatrical world, in politics, guerrilla warfare and crisis situations, provided the leader is good – for they talk of leaders rather than managers in these cultures. They are a *convenient* way of running things, although not necessarily the best, when the core organization is small (under twenty people perhaps) and closely gathered together so that personal communication is easy. Once things get much bigger than that, formality has to be increased, and the personal, telepathic empathetic style is frustrated. The key to success is having the right people, who blend with the core team and can act on their own; therefore a lot of time is spent on selecting the right people and assessing whether they will fit in or not. It is no accident that some of the most successful club cultures have a nepotistic feel to them; they deliberately recruit people like themselves, even from the same family, so that the club remains a club.

The role culture

It is all very different in a role culture. The best picture of a role culture is the kind of organization chart that these organizations all have. It looks like a pyramid of boxes; inside each box is a job title with an individual's name in smaller type below, indicating that she or he is currently the occupant of that box, but of course the box continues even if the individual departs. The boxes fit into departmental pillars, which are then co-ordinated at the top, rather like a Greek temple.

Figure 11

The 'organizational idea' behind this type of culture is that organizations are sets of *roles* or job-boxes, joined together in a logical and orderly fashion so that together they discharge the work of the organization. The organization is a piece of construction engineering, with role piled on role, and responsibility linked to responsibility. Individuals are 'role occupants' with job descriptions that effectively lay down the requirements of the role and its boundaries. From time to time, the organization will rearrange the roles and their relationship to each other, as priorities change, and then re-allocate the individuals to the roles.

The communications in these cultures are formalized, as are the systems and procedures. The memoranda go from role to role ('Head of *X* Dept' to 'Deputy Head') and are copied to roles, not individuals. The place abounds in procedures for every eventuality, in rules and handbooks; there are standards, quality controls and evaluation procedures. It is all organized and *managed* rather than led.

Most mature organizations have a lot of the role culture in them, because once an operation has settled down then it can be routinized and, as it were, imprinted on the future. All organizations strive for predictability and certainty; for then fewer decisions are needed, everybody can get on with their job, the outcomes can be guaranteed, and the inputs calculated. You know where you are and where you will be; it is secure and comfortable even if it is at times too predictable to be exciting.

These role organizations thrive when they are doing a routine, stable and unchanging task, but they find it hard to cope with change or with individual exceptions. If it's not in the rule book they really have to wait for the rule book to be rewritten before they can act. Administrative organizations, as in part of the social security system, *have* to be role cultures and they will prove very frustrating if you turn out to be one of those individual exceptions. On the other hand, if the social security system were administered by a host of club cultures, each responding as they saw fit, social justice would hardly be served. Efficiency and fairness in routine tasks demand a role culture.

The important thing in these cultures is to get the logic of the design right, the flow of work and the procedures. People are, in one sense, a less critical factor. They can be trained to fit the role. Indeed role cultures do not want too much independence or initiative. Railways want train drivers to arrive on time, not five minutes early. Role cultures want 'role occupants' not individualists.

The task culture

The task culture evolved because of the need for an organizational form that could respond to change in a less individualistic way than a club culture, and more speedily than a role culture. The 'organizational idea' of this culture is that a group or team of talents and resources should be applied to a project, problem or task. In that way each task gets the treatment it requires – it does not have to be standardized across the organization – and the groups can be changed, disbanded or increased as the task changes. A net, which can pull its cords this way and that and regroup at will, is the picture of this culture.

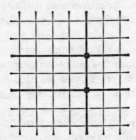

Figure 12

This is the preferred culture of many competent people, because they work in groups, sharing both skills and responsibilities. They are constantly working on new challenges since every task is different, and they thus keep themselves developing and enthused. The task culture is usually a warm and friendly culture because it is built around co-operative groups of colleagues without much overt hierarchy. There are plans rather than procedures, reviews of progress rather than assessment of past performance. It is a forward-looking culture for a developing organization.

These cultures thrive in situations where *problem-solving* is the job of the organization. Consultancy, advertising agencies, construction work, parts of journalism and the media, product development groups, surgical teams: any situation that is beyond the capacity of one man or one woman and their minions to solve, and which cannot be proceduralized or automated, needs a task culture.

The problem is that these cultures are expensive. They use professional competent people who spend relatively a lot of time talking together in search of the right solution. You would not use a task culture to make a wheel because they really *would* want to re-invent it, or at least improve on it, first. It is a questioning culture, which chafes at routines and the daily grind of 'administration' or 'repetitive chores'. A task culture talks of 'co-ordinators' and 'team leaders' rather than managers; it is full of budgets (which are plans) but short on job descriptions; it wants commitment and it rewards success with more assignments. It promises excitement and challenge but not security of employment because it cannot afford to employ people who do not continually meet new challenges successfully. Task cultures, therefore, tend to be full of young energetic people developing and testing talents, people who are self-confident enough not to worry about long-term security – at least until they are older.

The person culture

The person culture is very different from all the previous three. The other three cultures put the organization's purposes first and then, in their different ways, harness the individual to this purpose. The person culture puts the individual first and makes the organization the resource for the individual's talents. The most obvious examples are doctors, who for their own convenience group themselves in a practice, barristers in chambers (a very minimal sort of organization), architects in partnerships, artists in a studio, and perhaps professors in faculties or scientists in a research laboratory.

The 'organizational idea' behind this culture is that the individual talent is all-important and must be serviced by some sort of minimal organization. Adherents do not in fact like to use the word 'organization' but find all sorts of alternative words ('practice', 'chambers', 'partnership', 'faculty', etc.') instead. Nor do they talk of 'managers' but of 'secretaries', 'bursars', 'chief clerk', etc.; indeed the 'managers' of these organizations are always lower in status than the professionals. You may have a 'senior partner' in a law office but if you ask for the 'manager' you are likely to be shown in to the chief clerk. Stars, loosely grouped in a cluster or constellation, are the image of a person culture.

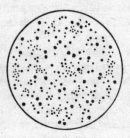

Figure 13

The individual professionals in these organizations usually have tenure, meaning that the management is not only lower in status but has few if any formal means of control over the professionals. In a university, for these reasons, the head of department or the dean of a faculty is usually a rotating job, often seen as a necessary chore rather than a mark of distinction.

In other words, a person culture is very difficult to run in any ordinary way. The professionals have to be run on a very light rein. They can be persuaded, not commanded; influenced, cajoled or bargained with, but not managed. The only kind of power that counts is therefore expert or personal power, because the 'stars' are effectively protected against anything that the holders of the resources or the formal authority can do.

The person culture works where the talent of the individual is what matters, which is why you find it in the old professions, or in the arts, some sports and some religions. Increasingly however some professions are finding that the problems are too complex for one individual's talents. Architects, city solicitors, even the clergy are grouping themselves into task cultures and submitting themselves to more organizational disciplines. Clusters are needed, not individual stars – but clusters involve a loss of autonomy and a willingness to work with others, a different kind of culture.

The mix of cultures

These are the pure forms of the cultures, but few organizations have only one culture. They are more often a mix of all four. What makes each organization different is the mix that they choose. What makes them successful is, often, getting the right mix at the right time.

That is not easy, because organizations are people and people have their own cultural preferences and inclinations. Whatever we may think we are usually predisposed to one culture with another back-up culture as a possible alternative, but someone who is at home in a role culture will be incapacitated in the more intuitive free-form atmosphere of a club culture, and vice versa. Thus role cultures, for example, find it hard to change themselves into task cultures even if percipient leaders see that such a change is necessary. They often need a blood transfusion of new people if the culture is really going to change, and that, of course, is what tends to happen in the more cut-and-thrust world of business organizations. Where such dramatic transfusions are impossible, organizations tend to play around with the structure, partly to bring new people into prominence, partly to give themselves the freedom to set new norms of behaviour – that is, to introduce a new culture.

The mix that you end up with at any one time is influenced by the following factors:

Size. Large size and role cultures go together. The theorists are still arguing about which causes which. Is a bureaucracy a bureaucracy because it is large and because that is the only way to organize a thousand or more people? Or is it large because it is a bureaucracy, because that is the only way to manage a complicated task and it has to be large to justify all the overheads of bureaucracy? This is a pertinent question for the education system, which is happy to group children under 11 in small units but wants units of four to five times the size when they are aged 12 to 18. The other, non-role cultures can operate only where the core staff number less than thirty or so.

Work-flow. The way the work is organized has an important bearing on the culture you can operate. If it is organized in separate units or 'job-shops' where a group or an individual can be responsible for the whole job, then club, task or person cultures can exist. But if the work-flow is sequential or interdependent, in that one piece is tied in with another, then you need more systems, rules and regulations, and the culture shifts towards a role culture. In other words, a lot depends on what the job of the organization is seen to be. Primary schools have 'job-shops', secondary schools interdependent systems, as a general rule.

Environment. Every organization has to think about the raw material it receives and the products it turns out for society, whether those be bars of soap or educated human beings. If the environment does not give clear signals, if the institution is a monopoly and can therefore set its own goals and standards, or if the environment never changes, then the organization will tend to go for stability and a routine quiet life: a role culture. A changing or a demanding environment requires a culture that will respond to change: a task or club culture.

History. Organizations are to some extent stuck with their past, with their reputation, the kinds of people they hired years ago, their site and their traditions. These things take years if not decades to change. You have to start with what you've got, which is perhaps the hardest lesson for any enthusiastic headteacher to learn, as she or he dreams of all that might be. A staff accustomed to a club culture with a strong central figure will find it very hard to adjust to the more participative task culture even if they all claim that this is what they want. Old habits, particularly of dependency, die hard.

The cultural mix in any one organization depends on the relative importance of each of those factors. Often you will find a role culture topped by a spider's web with task-culture project groups round the edges and a few individuals of the person culture studded throughout like raisins in a cake. A consultancy group is different, however. There the dominant culture will be 'task', with sets of task groups held together by a small spider's web in the centre and a low-profile role culture doing the logistics and the accounts, in a service role. Some organizations are different again, being really federations or alliances of 'brains' – separate club cultures, in other words – loosely linked together by an administrative department or role culture, but largely free to do their own thing in their own way. There is no cultural blueprint for organizations. You choose your mix to fit your situation, bearing in mind that you have to start with what you've got, principally the people, who will each have their own cultural preferences.

What culture is a school?

The study by Handy suggested that the cultures apply to schools no less than to other organizations. Teachers, with few exceptions, saw themselves as task-culture *aficionados*. A very few preferred the person culture, and fewer still the club or the role culture. Teaching it seems is seen as a group activity by competent people dealing with a constantly changing challenge: the education of the young. Ideologically, the idea that education can be reduced to the systems and procedures of the role culture, the world of 'management', is rejected.

When teachers look at their organizations, however, the ideal is not always there, but there is a big difference between primary and secondary schools. The primary schools were scored on the questionnaires as almost pure task cultures, although observation would suggest that in some cases a benevolent club culture would have been a more appropriate description. They were small enough for either. Each teacher had their own 'job-shop' or year group, which interestingly was itself usually organized in task groups of children sitting in groups rather than rows. Communication between staff in primary schools is very personal and informal, even telepathic across the classroom or in the passageway.

Seondary schools on the other hand were scored with a predominance of the role culture. They were big, the work-flow was very interdependent, with the timetable or operations plan a major feature, responsibility was divided up by function (academic and pastoral, year tutor or subject teacher), and there were arrays of systems, co-ordinating procedures and committee meetings. Only the very junior teachers saw the secondary school as a person or task culture in which they were left alone to get on with their own thing. Those in the middle ranks also perceived there to be a club culture on top of the role culture, the head and her or his deputies: a web on top of the boxes.

The question has to be: does the role culture need to be so dominant in the secondary school? There are undoubtedly a large number of forces pushing it that way:

- Age-related, norm-referenced examinations push towards standardization of teaching.
- The felt need to offer a wide choice of subjects requires large numbers of teachers and therefore large numbers of students.
- Promotion possibilities, if tied at first to increasing proficiency in a subject area, encourage specialization by individuals and hierarchical organizations within the school.

- Trade unions press for the formalization of procedures and job demarcation.
- Education authorities look for financial economies of scale through large institutions.

A large institution, divided up into special functions, with a requirement that the functions combine to produce a standardized product, is thus inevitably going to have a preponderance of role-culture elements.

On the other hand, Richard Matthew and Simon Tong in their book *The Role of the Deputy Head in the Comprehensive School* describe a school as 'a series of interrelated independences', although they go on to suggest that 'the collegiate model will seem strange to many staffs and heads'. They see the school, in other words, as a *person culture* of individual professionals who have to be co-ordinated almost in spite of themselves. Within the role culture, a person culture bubbles away.

The traditions of professionalism remain strong in teaching. Tenure, the privacy of the classroom, the right to express one's own views in one's own way and the sense of accountability to one's profession – these are all the hallmarks of a profession and of a person culture. They do not sit well with graded hierarchies, standardized curricula and the management ethos of large institutions, all of which call for a role culture.

The secondary school today seems afflicted by a sort of organizational schizophrenia; is it a bureaucratic factory delivering goods or is it a collective of individual professionals each doing their own professional thing? It is convenient for governments, local authorities and parents to see it as a factory. Then they can ask it to deliver particular types of goods, they can use the language of resources and outputs, they can impose quality control and other regulations, they can measure and compare effectiveness.

The ethos of education, the development of the individual, the crucial interaction between individual teacher and individual pupil, by contrast, all argue for the maintenance of the professional tradition. Which should it be? It is not easy, perhaps not possible, to run a role culture stuffed full of person-culture professionals. Primary schools do not try. They remain task or club cultures, which can tolerate professionals as long as they are not outrageously independent. It has been accepted that primary schools stay small and sacrifice the economies and variety offered by large size. Was it a conscious decision?

If the school is to be an efficient role culture, then the traditions of the individualistic professions may have to be abandoned. The alternative is to move the schools towards task cultures, the half-way house to professionalism. This will require different philosophies of management from the ones currently prevailing in most secondary schools. Interestingly, however, modern businesses are moving away from hierarchies towards networks in response to the need for more flexibility and in order to give more room to the individual. It may be that in aping the bureaucracy of large businesses the secondary school has been adopting a theory of management that is already out of date.

Schools, like other organizations, are pulled four ways by the demands of the different cultures. Sometimes it must feel as if they are being pulled apart. Management's task is to gather the cultural forces together, using the strengths of each in the right places. It is not an easy task. It would be foolish therefore to ignore the lessons one can learn from the other organizations. The next chapter will explore these differences and similarities, in the belief that it may be unnecessary to 're-invent the wheel' in every school organization.

Structuring the organization

Systems of influence are fine and the cultures of organizations are revealing, but neither of them tells you precisely how to put the act together, how to arrange the individuals in their roles so that the place actually works. Here again it may be small comfort to be told that there is no sure way, but at least it is a licence to experiment. It may explain why schools, like most other organizations, are constantly adapting their structure or turning it upside down.

Structural change, provided that it is not an annual game of musical chairs, can be good in itself for the organization. People need new roles from time to time if they are to grow and develop as individuals and if the school, through them, is to grow and develop. Long familiarity with a role gradually builds up the set of 'demands' at the heart of the role and accepts more and more 'constraints', effectively squeezing out the area of choice in the eyes of the person in the role. 'No, it can't be done any differently' and 'I've always done it this way' are two of the verbal symptoms of a sitting tenant in a role, who ought to be moving on. If the school is not growing in size, if there is little turnover of staff, particularly in the middle, and if there is no noticeable change in its task, then an element of structural change is a good stimulant – one often indulged in, incidentally, by new headteachers who want to find some degrees of freedom.

But change to what? Are there any guiding principles? Yes, there seem to be some:

(1) Every organization needs its *core*, the operating group that is the focus of its work. This core is *serviced*, advised and co-ordinated by other groups, with information, material resources or people. The distinction is usually made between the 'line' (the core operating groups) and the 'staff' (the servicing and advisory groups). That sounds simple; but it is not always that easy, as we shall see, to decide what should be the line and what the staff.

(2) The structure must reflect the *diversity* of its task and of the population it is serving. A widely spread population needs a structure with a similar spread. In other words if a business produces one product for seventeen different regions it will have a structure with many regional branches. If it had three products it might add three product managers to the seventeen branch managers. Schools, as we shall see, have similar spreads, although they are called 'subjects' not 'products', 'age' or 'ability ranges' not 'branches'.

(3) The more diverse the structure the more *co-ordination* you need. One product to one area – a launderette, for instance – needs only minimal co-ordination, the man or woman on the spot. Add in some wine-bars and more launderettes in other parts of the country, and the one person can't do it. It sounds obvious, but it isn't easy to take the next step to delegation and co-ordination.

(4) It is *false economy* to use one structural element for many purposes. Some are bound to get neglected, particularly if they conflict.

Let us look at each element in turn.

The core unit ('line' and 'staff')

In a primary school the core unit is obviously the age group of pupils, with one teacher teaching all or most of the subjects, serviced perhaps by one or two specialist teachers or remedial units. It is clear who is in charge of the education of the child.

In a secondary school it is not always so clear whether it is the year group, the house, the form or the subject area that is the core unit. The school would normally say that it was the class or form, but in many schools this is a constantly changing group (depending on the subject), with no territory of its own, no group identity, no real leader who commands and co-ordinates its activities. To the outsider it can seem that it is the subject groups (i.e. the teachers) that are the core units, serviced by pupils and advised by pastoral staff. That may be an unfair or inaccurate assessment of most schools, but the fact that there is not an obvious core unit in some schools means that the structure is confusing; what is the driving force in the institution? Should the core unit be headed by staff with a more pastoral or broad educational mission or by staff who are essentially subject teachers? Not everyone can be both.

One is reminded of the organization of a typical double-glazing firm in which one person makes the sale, another takes the measurement, and a third fits the window in place. Logically this is fine, and if everyone does their job perfectly, and nothing changes in the meantime, it all works fine; but let one person err ever so slightly, let the customer change his or her mind, and it becomes impossible to find out who carries overall responsibility for the operation; in despair you ring the managing director. It can be the same with schools; where every bit locks together logically, who is in charge of the child's education? Who, in other words, is the line officer and who the staff?

Box 4.3 Territory

Territory can be a useful metaphor in organization structures. It can be defined psychologically as well as physically. People tend to regard their roles or their responsibilities as their personal territory (see the primary teachers in Chapter 1). No one, they feel, should enter the territory without permission, should certainly not rearrange the furniture or, worst of all, move in another tenant.

On the other hand, people take pride in their territory if they feel that they own it, and people deprived of territory can feel as aimless and homeless as stateless persons. Everyone needs a sense of their own territory in an organization if they are going to be an effective citizen. They will want the freedom to make that territory their own, by in some way imposing their own personality on it, as we redecorate the new home we have bought, even if it may not need it.

Psychological territory needs physical expression. We all need our own corner, and open-plan offices quickly get split into separate spaces divided up by filing cabinets and potted plants. In secondary schools teachers are quick to establish their territories, both psychological and physical, but it is not always obvious where the individual child finds his or her territory. Without psychological or physical space of their own children will look increasingly to a peer group or a gang, and will often get a sense of personal space from opposition to authority. Schools are foolish to neglect the importance of territory, for staff *or* for students.

Diversity

How do you reconcile different ages, different abilities and different interests in one structure? If you want to you can start by separating out the ages (year groups), then separating out the interests (options) and then separating out the abilities (streaming). The interesting decision is which separation comes first, because you will not end up in the same place irrespective of where you start. Schools seem to have universally decided that age is the first factor to be separated out. If they stop there they end up with mixed abilities and mixed interests in a common age-band. If Piaget is taken very seriously then there could be good educational grounds for this decision. Logically, however, it is only one of several possibilities. In further education the interests (i.e. subject choice) come first, followed by splitting the abilities if money allows, with age given small consideration. Community colleges often claim to find advantages in working with groups whose ages may be mixed but who share a common interest in a subject and have a similar range of ability; so do choirs, orchestras, drama groups. They sort by subject first, and pay less heed to age. The choice, in other words, is not inevitable.

Do schools, in their structure, reflect all the diversity that is required of them? The educational menu is vast if one looks at all the possibilities in an à la carte version. Schools have to offer a fixed menu, but it should vary with the times. More diversity does not necessarily mean more choice in the curriculum. It means more pressures from the structure on the core unit. A very complex business organization will have a product structure, a functional structure and a regional structure all bearing down on the person who has to deliver the goods. Schools should presumably be producing a range of different products (pupils) for a range of different markets (future lives), each with different specifications. That sort of diversity would suggest that there ought to be somebody in the structure with a vested interest in each type of product and market. Too often, it seems, only the up-market product is represented adequately in the structure.

Schools seem often to be structured as if they were a production organization producing an Identikit product for a mass market, which was greedily snapping up everything that came out. This, of course, as all schools know only too well, is not the true picture but it may be the bugbear of the ideology of equality. If they *were* a business they would have to appoint more product managers to reflect the diversity or they would go out of business. Perhaps it has to be so with schools, with more teachers taken away, if only for part of their time, from teaching the traditional subjects to supervising particular sorts of education for particular sorts of fortunes. When everyone is in the production line, no one is watching the market-place. That is all right if you have a monopoly, if you don't care, or if the world outside is totally uniform and unchanging. None of these things is true of education today.

Schools are in general not as complex in their structure as they probably ought to be, mainly because more complexity tends to mean more staff and therefore more money. If, however, for economic reasons diversity has to go unrecognized it is all the more important to be clear as to which priorities need to be given power in the structure. Schools probably have more choice than they think they have if they unlock themselves from their conditioned ways of thinking about organization.

Co-ordination

Differentiation must be matched by integration as the theoretical principle. Organizational theorists have described schools as 'loosely coupled' organizations in recognition of the large part played by the system of expertise in them and the resulting decentralization of day-to-day decisions (e.g. in the classroom); but even loosely coupled organizations need to be held together or they drift into anarchy.

There is an array of possible co-ordinating devices, most of them operating within the system of authority. The more diverse the tasks the more of these devices you will need. A primary school could probably make do with the first two, but a large comprehensive may well end up with all of them. Here they are:

- Direct contact by the superior.
- Rules and procedures.
- Appeals to the hierarchy.
- Temporary co-ordinating groups (project teams).
- Permanent co-ordinating groups (committees).
- Individual co-ordinators.
- Co-ordinating departments.

Co-ordinators, however, have a difficult job. Their formal authority is often not enough to do the job properly; they also need to have a personal credibility, or expert power, if they are going to get the full co-operation of all concerned. They also will need to call on considerable interpersonal skills. It is not, therefore, a job for a new young member of staff, nor for an old one who has passed her or his best.

False economy

It is tempting to say, 'Since we already have a committee why does it not also . . .?' It is easier to say to a science teacher, 'Please also make sure that you develop their skills in presentation', than to set up a separate mechanism to do that. It is seductive to believe that you can, in the one interview, be judge, counsellor and target-setter to your junior. On the whole, however, it has proved to be better to find separate ways and times to do each.

Overburdening any part of the structure inevitably creates either role conflict or role overload for the individuals concerned. If they are not to start practising some of the coping mechanisms listed in Chapter 3 they will, unconsciously or consciously, drop off one or more of their role requirements. Because judges cannot be counsellors in the same meeting, we choose to be one or the other and end up too judgemental or too conciliatory. It is a false economy.

This is not to say that one person cannot do two jobs, or one group have a cluster of responsibilities. They can, *if* they consciously put each responsibility or task into a separate *territory*. A committee, for instance, faced with the task of (a) sharing routine progress reports and (b) brainstorming about the future of the school would be wise either to have separate meetings, with different seating arrangements, for each, or at least to have a break for tea in the middle so that people can adjust to their new roles and to new relationships with their colleagues.

Untidy structures are not a bad thing. They mean that there are many forces at work but also lots of checks and balances. If the organization is too neat, too logical, it often means that the task has been over-simplified and that something is being neglected.

Putting an organization together is therefore one of those never-finished tasks. You cannot do it without having a very clear idea of what the job or jobs of the organization are. Form, as they say, follows function. Equally, it is no good drawing lovely lines on paper if you do not have the people to put in the boxes or the systems of power that will bring those boxes to life. That is why, in any book on organizations, structure tends to come last although it often has to come first in life. You can't do it properly until you understand the rest. A school is not an engineering model; it is a city-state with citizens, with passions and factions, dreams and fears.

Leavitt uses a picture of a diamond (Figure 14) that is so simple you might take it for granted, but it is a remarkably useful reminder to those engaged in designing or changing organizations. It is intended to remind us that you can't change one without changing the others and that therefore each factor has a blocking power over the others. Before you change anything, work out the implications on the rest of the diamond.

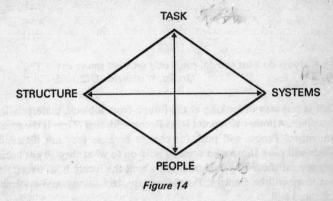

Figure 14

Some, for instance, think instinctively of *people* if there is a need to change anything. Get new people, change people round, develop others, get rid of some. Such individuals are often club-culture types. Others, from the role culture, start playing with the structure or the systems, setting up new committees or departments, changing houses into year groups or vice versa. Others prefer, in the task-culture tradition, to change the objectives or tasks of the groups or the institution. All of them, in the end, will have to deal with each. True leadership is knowing which one is best to start with, this time with this problem in this organization; for, as Heraclitus said of rivers, you can never step into precisely the same organization twice. That is the fun of it.

5 Facing the Future

If you always do what you do, you'll only get what you've got.
Graffiti, Washington DC, 1985

That is one way of looking at the future: from a black, underprivileged viewpoint. Another viewpoint is, as Bacon said, that 'Time is the greatest innovator.' People will push for change because they are dissatisfied; events will push those who want to hold on to what they've got because they are satisfied. The only certainty about the future is its uncertainty, that there will be changes. People, society, technology, eco-systems do not stand still.

Organizations cannot stand still either. Those that wish to thrive, or even survive, have to change in tune with the society around them. One view of progress in Britain could be that institutions do *not* change, they merely wither away allowing new ones to replace them. The changing names in the high streets lend some support to that view, but there is no inevitability about it. Organizations *can* adapt, if they decide to do so. Schools will need to adapt or, unbelievably, they might wither away, their functions taken over by other bodies. By 1985, for instance, the Manpower Services Commission was already spending nearly as much on training as the whole of the further education sector of the UK.

Taking a forward viewpoint is, therefore, part of the role of any leader or management group. All large companies have a research-and-development group or a market intelligence unit. It is natural to assume that your product is sound and your markets certain when your goods are selling well. But, as many British companies found in the 1970s, markets, costs and technology can change rapidly and catch you out. Jaguar Cars survived then only by a supreme effort – by reappraising their product, technology, ways of working and markets. They now telephone five hundred customers a month around the world to get comments on performance and faults. This information is then fed back into the production system, and the organization adapts.

A surprising feature of the education service is how little operational or market research is carried out at the grass-roots level. Few local education authorities engage in research or have a forward-planning unit. Fewer schools or colleges engage systematically in market intelligence. Many would consider that their noses are too close to the grindstone to be able to sniff the air for new winds.

Predicting the future is a hazardous business. You can so easily be wrong or only half-right because the pace and effects were different from what you saw, or because an unforeseen development turned up out of the blue. Daring to think forward carries risks – including that you might be ridiculed. Nevertheless we propose in this chapter to be foolhardy, on the assumption that if you, the reader, reject our interpretation – which is quite likely – you will be stirred to some projections of your own.

The problem need not be as difficult as it seems. Just as the present has grown out of the past, so the future grows out of the present. Reasonable predictions can be made from present trends. The difficulty lies in spotting the winners; that is, winnowing those trends that will intensify from those that will die away, blowing the wheat from the chaff.

We propose to do this under three main headings:

● The market.
● The product.
● Delivery.

These terms may seem too unfamiliar, too harsh to use in a consideration of schools and the needs of children. But we think this approach may yield interesting results, with *clues* to the ways in which schools may have to change. Anticipating the future has a purpose only (other than as an armchair guessing-game) if it leads to an organizational response. It will be clear that much of what is already happening and is likely to happen will change schooling almost beyond recognition. If our current schools wish to be part of the action they will need to change. If they don't, we believe, they will be allowed to wither while other institutions pick up the challenge. The future has to be a present concern.

The market

In industry and commerce the customers are those who see a benefit in purchasing a product or in using a service. If they don't like it or do not feel a need for it they won't buy it. To boost their sales, firms do a lot of persuading and reading of public tastes to maintain or increase their 'share of the market'. And they need to see that they are not upstaged by rival firms with more attractive products. Competition is the motivating adrenalin in this productive system.

It is a perennial question as to whether or how far this can apply in the public sector and particularly in the personal services. A society defines the customers of these services by Acts of Government. So, in Britain, all children aged between 5 and 16 are required to receive education. The great majority attend their local publicly provided schools whether they want to or not. They are captive customers.

The staff of a school have the task of deciding how to provide for all without discrimination: the principle of equality of opportunity. In order to be able to do this, headteachers and their staffs need to have a view of what education is to be provided; that is, what are the opportunities that they are trying to provide equally? In this way the aims and content of education are generalized; the norm becomes the standard currency of the system. The individual needs of customers tend to be subsumed in the general provision. Bespoke tailoring is ousted by ready-to-wear mass production.

But is the reality as simple and static as this would seem to suggest? Are the schools assured of their market, and are their 'captive' customers content to receive education passively? Are children necessarily the only customers, or are there others in society seeking school-*level* education or for whom schools could provide? Looking at the education market more closely, we discern four processes that seem to be occurring:

- Traditional client groups are changing.
- Traditional customers have new needs.
- There are 'new customers'.
- Values affecting the way people are educated are changing.

Traditional clients

The first and obvious change is that there are fewer children. It is a phenomenon evident in all advanced nations that the birth rate fell by as much as 30 per cent between the 1960s and 1980. So school systems, which had expanded to cope with the 'baby boom', are now faced with empty places and the traumas of schools being closed or amalgamated.

But this is being accompanied by other trends provoked by social and economic factors. There is a growing demand for earlier schooling: for more kindergarten or nursery provision. At the other end, more school students want to extend their education beyond the statutory leaving age. The Soviet Union raised its school-leaving age by a year in 1978; in

North America the *majority* continue their studies at high school or college to age 21; in West Germany 86 per cent stay on to 18, and 96 per cent do so in Japan.

A noticeable feature of the British system has been that the school-leaving age has been raised only when more than 50 per cent of students were staying on voluntarily. Are we approaching that position again (47 per cent in 1986)? Or have we passed it – since in effect all those who leave school at sixteen are guaranteed training for a further two years by the Youth Training Scheme?

New needs of traditional customers

The 'profile' of children within the traditional school age range is also changing. There are more children in mainstream schools of different racial origins, with various disabilities or with different or difficult social backgrounds.

The world is shrinking; there is now much greater mobility between countries and continents and therefore rubbing of shoulders and minds between peoples. British membership of the European Community is continually producing comparisons between practice and principles in the member states. There are considerable numbers of workers in Britain who come from countries in the EEC. The arrival of Commonwealth immigrants in Britain has produced, among them and their descendants, new dimensions of cultural variety in language, religion, dress, manners, values, festivals, music, art, literature, marriage and family patterns.

There are significant changes too in attitudes towards education of children with disabilities or learning difficulties. In Britain the category 'ineducable' was withdrawn in 1972, and those children who were until then looked after by the local health service became the responsbility of the education service as *schoolchildren*. In 1978 the Warnock Committee reported on its review of *The Education of Handicapped Children and Young People*. The main impact of Warnock is threefold:

- that we should stop fitting children to predetermined categories and should instead identify and provide for each child's learning needs;
- that there are many more children – as many as 20 per cent of an age group – who have learning difficulties and special needs;
- that parents' (and by implication students') involvement in the identification and provision for special needs should be made more explicit.

Bespoke tailoring is on the way back! All schools in future will be involved in providing for special needs. The present separation between special and mainstream education will become more and more blurred. The requirement to respond specifically to a student's learning needs is likely to have a ripple effect on method and attitudes throughout mainstream schooling and across the ability range.

This is also reflected in the considerable volume of human rights legislation, which was a feature of the late 1960s and 1970s: including that relating to disabled persons, mental health, equality between sexes, racial groups, homosexuals, children and young people. The effects of such legislation are expressed only gradually in everyday practice. We can expect further pressures for the rights or needs of individuals to be met in school programmes; especially in terms of language and culture, and of equal opportunity between races and the sexes.

In 1980 parents were given more say in the education of their children. Schools now have to issue annually a prospectus giving details of the curriculum, the choices that are available and examination courses and results. Parents have the right to express a choice about curriculum options and which school they wish their child to attend. They have the right of appeal if their choice is not met. Parents are now represented on all school governing bodies.

Since the general level of education and qualifications is rising, it can be expected that parents will express their views more often and more articulately. Teachers know, and there is research evidence to show, that parents expect at least as high a level of education for their children as they received themselves. The cultural expectations of the family are shifted by education.

Family patterns are changing too. In Britain the number of divorces rose from 74,000 in 1971 to 148,000 in 1980, and abortions from 50,000 in 1969 to 130,000 in 1980. It is predicted that 1 in 3 children will experience a one-parent family situation at some time during their childhood (60 per cent of divorces involve children under sixteen).

In his book *Future Shock* the US sociologist Alvin Toffler puts such trends down to 'the accelerative thrust of technology . . . whereby we are exchanging things, places, ideas, organisations and people more rapidly in our lives'. All advanced technological societies are showing increases in tension, unrest and breakdown within communities, families and individuals.

The Scarman Report on the 1981 troubles in Brixton and the little noticed Home Office Report, *Public Disorder*, on the unrest in Handsworth, Birmingham, in 1981, both refer to the boredom and sense of alienation and rejection felt by sections of the community, par-ticularly the young. Many of these young people are still at school; many have been before the courts (a $7\frac{1}{2}$ per cent increase in juvenile crime between 1972 and 1982); many are on probation or under supervision. Increasingly local health and social services are withdrawing from the full-time care of children – in hospital or community homes – and are instead supporting such youngsters in the care of their families (domiciliary care) or with foster parents. As a result more children who require particular help are staying in the school system, thus intensifying schools' problems in meeting special needs.

A senior member of H M I, the schools inspectorate, has spoken of the 'baffling ambiguity of human existence'. School systems need to consider this in the context of the young who will live most of their lives in the twenty-first century. They will have to live in an age characterized by accelerating change.

One of the most pervasive changes is taking place in the world of work. We have moved from a majority being employed in blue-collar occupations to a predominance of white-collar jobs. The context of employment is changing. It can rarely be expected now that training for an occupation on leaving school will last for a working lifetime. Retraining for new skills, change of occupation, periods of unemployment and more self-employment are the more likely patterns of the future. Indeed work is becoming less dominant in people's lives. The working lifetime, year, week and day is shortening.

For the young, about to embark on an adult life, this can be baffling and frustrating. Their access to the adult employment market is more difficult, slower in coming. In many areas of Britain barely 10 per cent of those who leave school at sixteen go directly into permanent jobs. Many have not had regular employment by the age of twenty. It is no longer sufficient to gain academic qualifications at age sixteen. They are no longer a passport to a job. This presents schools with a challenge; what more can be offered to help the students both beyond age sixteen *and before*? The challenge includes a gauntlet being thrown at the curriculum. There are demands for more practical skills, more technical and vocational experience, and there is a growing demand that social and personal competence – 'life skills' – should be included in school programmes.

New customers

The appetite for education is growing, at all levels in society. This trend will surely intensify, particularly in combination with three other developments:

- People are living longer.
- Work (i.e. paid employment) is taking up less time in people's lives.
- Information technology is making knowledge more accessible.

Individuals have, and will have, more time on their hands: leisure time, unprogrammed time, time at their command to express themselves as they wish. How will they want to use it?

There is no simple or single answer. Some seek additional work by 'moonlighting' or odd-jobbing or in do-it-yourself. Others seek opportunities through voluntary work, including for example those (25,100) who act as tutors in the adult literacy programme or in the Youth Service (523,000 voluntary youth leaders). There is also a powerful trend towards more active, purposeful use of leisure time: in sport and fitness, cookery, art, crafts, music, travel, car maintenance, wine-making, use of computers, drama, photography, etc.

Many of these activities take place on school premises, outside school hours, through adult education programmes and through local interest or community groups. Often the school and other uses are kept separate, but increasingly such activities are coming together with schools being designated as 'community' schools or colleges. Some areas – Cambridgeshire, Leicestershire, Coventry – have pushed this wheel with the shoulder of a deeper philosophy. Henry Morris in the 1930s was deeply concerned at the flight from the villages of Cambridgeshire to the towns and the danger that the culture and life of the countryside would be lost:

> The Village College would change the whole face of the problem of rural education. As the community centre for the neighbourhood it would provide for the whole man ... it would not only be a training ground for the art of living but the place where life is lived, the environment of a genuine corporate life ... there would be no 'leaving school'; the child would enter at three and leave only in extreme old age.
>
> *The Henry Morris Collection*, ed. H. Rée, 1984, p. 28

In 1982 the City of Coventry declared that 'education is a lifelong process' and should be available at all levels and ages – when, where, how and what people wanted. All the secondary schools in the city are being developed also as 'community colleges' – large community centres within which there is a day school – open for fourteen hours a day, 6 or 7 days a week. One such inner-city community college is used by 140,000 people a year for non-school activities. Nine hundred adults – mainly parents – are attending Coventry primary schools during the day to qualify in school-level subjects. These are large numbers, indicating something more than a fringe activity.

Colin Fletcher's report, *The Challenges of Community Education* (Department of Education, University of Nottingham, 1983) indicated similar developments at Sutton in Ashfield, Nottinghamshire, where 300,000 people are using the centre a year (though see also Fletcher's book *Schools on Trial* for some of the difficulties encountered by community colleges). There are many other emerging initiatives, for example in Liverpool, Hounslow, Newham and Newcastle-upon-Tyne. The Community Education Development Centre led by John Rennie has a membership of over one thousand schools and is involved with more than thirty education authorities in England who are interested in developing similar programmes. The Secondary Heads' Association has likewise (1984) declared:

Schools may need to develop as centres for learning for people of all ages, i.e. as community schools in which adults young and old, in or out of work, attend courses for pleasure, for retraining, for leisure or to share their skills with others. In this case the existing conventions of the timing of the school and the holidays become even more inappropriate; equally the segregation of the adolescent age group for learning purposes ceases to be either necessary or appropriate.

A View from the Bridge, SHA, 1984

So if (at last) education is coming to be seen and practised as a lifelong process, what is the role of schools in provision for this? Can they, should they, see themselves as local learning, culture and leisure centres for the whole community? Is the adult market part of their market in the future?

If learning involves all of one's life ... then we must go even further than the necessary overhaul of 'educational systems' until we reach the stage of a learning society. For these are the true proportions of the challenge education will be facing in the future.

UNESCO Report, *Learning to Be*, 1972

Changing values

'The customer is always right' is a much used slogan in industry and commerce. Often one can doubt its validity in practice. Producers can stimulate their own markets by efficient advertising and selling or by cartels or scarcity. 'Big business' can so dominate a market as to have a virtual monopoly and thereby dictate consumer tastes. In which case it is rather a matter of the producer knowing best what the customer needs because that is what he can produce!

But there are increasing signs of human reaction against such assumptions, against being typed. There is more demand for out-of-the-ordinary things; for standard products to be 'customized' (e.g. cars). People want to express their individuality more, their uniqueness – perhaps as a way of wresting more control over their lives in an increasingly complex, interdependent society. There is more protection for the customer under legislation than ever before. There are signs of a greater regard for the individual in both product design and methods of production. 'Small is beautiful'; the seeds of decay in mass production, mass consumerism are showing.

Education for the masses, comprehensive education, is showing symptoms of the same trends. When Disraeli declared in 1867, 'Upon the education of the people of this country the future of this country depends', he was more concerned about *his* future since the masses now had the right to vote. He was speaking in the high summer of Victorian paternalism when children were to be 'seen and not heard' and educated 'according to their station in life'. But when a society decides that all children shall be educated it raises some fundamental issues and powerful questions, such as:

- What is education for? Is it for the benefit of the children or for the benefit of society?
- What should be the content of education?
- How are children to be educated? In what sort of environment?

The answers to such questions depend upon what is valued by society and how that society values its children. The influences shaping these values comes from the depths of society's cultural inheritance.

Some of the most powerful influences that have shaped the views of western societies are:

- The stock of philosophical ideas, such as those coming down to us from the Greeks (the thinker is superior to the craftsman); Locke (the mind as a clean slate); Descartes (the value of the intellect and deductive scientific method); puritanism (the moral value of work and discipline).
- Psychological ideas, which presented a fixed hierarchical view of human ability (Burt), intelligence quotients (Binet), faculty psychology (Spearman).

The product of such influences has been a deeply engrained *paternalism* in school systems. Adults know best. Children should be educated 'according to their ages, abilities and aptitudes' (1944 Education Act) – which is not far removed from the Victorian 'according to their station in life', and was based on Burt psychology. Academic knowledge is superior to practical competence. Logic and analysis are superior to intuition and creative flair. The intelligence expected of the young is the intelligence of the intellect rather than also the intelligence of feelings; or as James Hemming puts it, 'thinking about abstractions rather than thinking from within' (*The Betrayal of Youth*).

But times change. The implications of the 'accelerative thrust of technology' are probably more far reaching for education systems than for any other organized aspect of society, for two reasons. First, electronic technology is accelerating the processing of information. Knowledge and facts are being exchanged so rapidly that this is increasing the development of new knowledge. Ideas are outdated more quickly. Secondly, universal access to television, microcomputer links, video tapes and computerized learning systems reduces the dependence upon the teacher to impart knowledge.

Kjell Eide, of the Norwegian Ministry of Education, sums the position up in this way:

Traditionally, educational institutions have not only been a prime source of socially accepted authoritative information to young people: they have also been the main judges of what information is appropriate and relevant for them ... Educational institutions have already lost this position ... other sources, often more easily available, provide contradictory information, structured in different ways and claiming the same degree of authority. Instead of forcing on pupils its view of what is right and what is relevant, the school in future can maintain its position as a useful agent to young people only in teaching them how to select and judge information in terms of their own interests and value premisses.

In other words, we have to help our young to cope with the 'baffling ambiguity' of human existence in an increasingly baffling, changing environment. This means shedding outworn ideologies and replacing them with new approaches. Education for the future is likely to be less about subjects and gathering knowledge and more about learning to live as an independently functioning being who is both self-regarding and regardful of others. That is, education will be more concerned with the growth of the whole person and the building of self-esteem based on Rogerian psychological ideas. The teacher's role is likely to be less didactic, less judgemental and more enabling and facilitating.

This also means a move away from the currency of the norm and the belief that a fixed general curriculum for all is equivalent to equal opportunity for all. If all children were to eat the same food they would still grow differently. The needs of the individual have to be met. 'The solutions . . . lie in co-operation with what the young *are*' (Hemming). We need more 'customized' education.

The product

The individual's entire life is nothing but a process of giving birth to himself: in truth we are only fully born when we die.

Erich Fromm, quoted in Faure Report, UNESCO, 1972

In industry, 'products' are a wide range of manufactured articles many of which are in everyday usage: machinery, electronic apparatus, furniture, food, chemicals, textiles and clothing, buildings. As such the outcomes of their activities are 'visible' and readily known in terms of quality, quantity and suitability. The products of commerce are less tangible because many commercial activities are concerned with providing services: banking, insurance, retailing, professional expertise. None the less such services are generally known and are quantifiable in the sense that they are directly experienced, immediate and on the whole short term.

The product of education has few of those characteristics. Essentially it is both invisible and long term. The product of education is *a process in the human being*: a process of growth within a person – of the whole person. Since humans are such complex beings, the processes of their education are complex. Indeed can we really define when a person is truly and wholly 'grown up'? As the Chinese have shown us, truths about human affairs are often best expressed as a paradox. Perhaps the only acceptable definition of an educated person is 'one who is still learning'.

Little wonder then that, in schooling systems that have to cater for *all* children, the complexity is simplified and reduced to more manageable, everyday terms. Since mass schooling began in the nineteenth century it is not surprising that the philosophical and psychological ideas outlined in the previous section strongly influenced how children should be educated. Ideas of mass production were copied, especially since teachers (i.e. people with the knowledge to pass on) were in short supply. Also, because books and language were then the only currency for the transmission of ideas, the system became heavily reliant upon them.

As a result a convention was established in school systems whereby the process of education had the following characteristics:

- *Method was didactic*. Children were collected together in groups (classes) to receive instructions from an expert (the teacher).
- *Content was intellectual*. It dealt with knowledge and cognitive skills through academic subjects (initially the 'three *R*'s').
- *Style was language-based*, as a vehicle for both instruction and learning.
- *Motivation was competitive*. Pupils were graded against the average for the class or age group.
- *Values were adult*, i.e. based on what adults decided children should know and do.

This crude reduction of the education process has been described as 'filling pitchers rather than lighting fires' or 'the mug-and-jug approach', whereby the teacher (the jug) possesses the intellectual and factual knowledge and causes the student to be the passive recipient (the mug) so that the knowledge can be poured in. It has had far-reaching consequences: most notably that *the product of the education process has come to be equated with how much knowledge a student can regurgitate*.

There are other powerful consequences or traditions that have been inherited. Some of the most important are concerned with:

- *Role and status*. The teacher rules by authority: choosing, directing, controlling and judging the learner's activities. The student is inferior, expected to be passive, obedient, without choice.
- *Classroom climate*. Enshrines a pecking order (by marks or remarks, 'good', 'fair', 'weak'); favours the conformist and denies sharing or any real development of group skills.
- *Content*. Concerned overwhelmingly with cognitive development and not also with affective, intuitive intelligence; concentrates on left-brain functions; is not concerned with the education of the whole person.

Most schools have moved away significantly from these beginnings. But traditions die hard, and there is still evidence of these characteristics in our schools. We have moved to a more child-centred and active learning approach, particularly in special and primary schools. The emphasis nevertheless remains on cognitive rather than affective development and on teaching rather than learning. This is especially the case in secondary schools, where the curriculum is still dominated by academic subjects and didactic method and is as a cart harnessed to the horse of the norm-based examination system.

The tradition that lives on most persistently, however, is in the relationship between teacher and pupils. The teacher dominates; pupils are

The cortex function as illustrated:

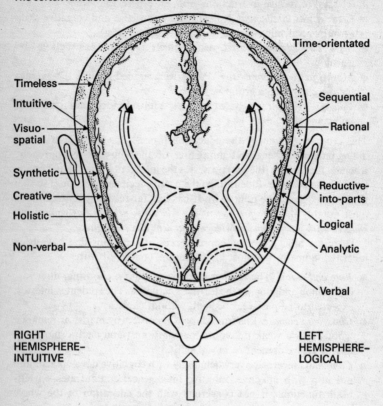

'Man's highest achievements stem from the successful integration of both left-brain intellect and right-brain intuition.'

Figure 15

Source: Primary Education Matters, published by Somerset Education Department, 1984.

subordinates. The teacher is the professional dealing all the cards, deciding and controlling what is to be learnt and done, how and when. This denies or sets aside the strengths, interests and experience of the students and the group – including their ability to make decisions and to evaluate their own learning.

Figure 16
The relative weight of influence on learning in a traditional classroom

It is this aspect of the product of education that is so inadequate and led David Hargreaves to declare so strongly that 'schooling damages dignity'. If the process of schooling is so dominated by adult authority, it is down-putting and rejectful of the individual and the group, and is likely to breed alienation and resentment, or dependency and conformity. It stunts the process of growth within a person by damaging self-esteem. This is the inner bastion of traditional education, which has yet to fall; change in the teacher/learner relationship is essential and urgent if we are to release our young with the inner strengths to cope with their future.

Box 5.1

We are living in the time of the parenthesis, the time between eras. It is as though we have bracketed off the present from both the past and the future, for we are neither here nor there ... Those who are willing to handle the ambiguity of this in-between period and to anticipate the new era will be a quantum leap ahead of those who hold on to the past. The time of the parenthesis is a time of change and questioning.

John Naisbitt, *Megatrends*, 1983

Change in the teacher/learner relationship is urgent because the future of young people is so full of ambiguities, uncertainty and change. How will they be able to pick their way through life – choosing their own attitude in any given set of circumstances, choosing their own way? There is ample evidence of stress and group pressures on individuals in society; Carl Rogers says in *Freedom to Learn for the Eighties*:

Individuals who tended to yield, agree, conform, the ones who could be controlled, gave general evidence of incapacity to cope effectively with stress, while the non-conformists did not tend to panic when placed under pressure of conflicting forces.

The conformists tended to have pronounced feelings of personal inferiority and inadequacy . . . to show a lack of openness and freedom in emotional processes. They were emotionally restricted, lacking in spontaneity, tending to repress their own impulses . . . The person who did not yield to pressure had a sense of competence and personal adequacy – was more self-contained and autonomous, a better judge of the attitudes of other people, free from pretence and unaffected. Where the conformist tended to lack insight into his/her own motives and behaviour, the independent person had a good understanding of self . . .

[This] seems to imply that the person who is free within him/herself, who is open to her/his experiences, who has a sense of her/his own freedom and responsible choice, is not nearly so likely to be controlled by his/her environment as is the person who lacks these qualities.

The competences and knowledge that young people need to exist in the adult world, now and in the future have been summarized in a working document (*Education for Transition: The Curriculum Challenge*) from the European Community, Brussels, in July 1984:

Individual or personal competences
- Self-knowledge – strengths/weaknesses, mental and physical.
- Self-confidence and autonomy.
- Ability to accept and use criticism.
- Initiatives.
- Logical capacity – decision-making, problem-solving.
- Living with emotions.
- Understanding and development of physical/health capacities.
- Development of manual skills.

Interpersonal competences
- Understanding of, and feeling for, others.
- Ability to discipline oneself to accept the rules of a group or an organization.
- Ability to co-operate with others in a common task.

- Ability to articulate ideas in words and to communicate, to listen, to explain, to argue, to read and to write.

Understanding and knowledge

- Understanding of number and basic mathematics.
- Understanding and knowledge of existing kinds of work, and of the organization of industry, commerce and administration; and of possible developments in the future, especially areas such as information technologies; and of the implications for the kind of personal and interpersonal competences needed.
- Understanding and knowledge of the alternative forms and patterns of human activity that might replace 'work', and of leisure activities.
- Understanding and knowledge of the nature of personal and family relationships.
- Understanding and knowledge of society as a whole and the individual's role in it.

There is a mounting tide of opinion flowing in the same direction and an increasing volume of corresponding practice among teachers.

The National Curriculum appeared on the face of it to run counter to these ideas, substituting subjects for competences. As the curriculum develops in practice, however, the concept of individual competences re-emerges. A significant example of the way the tide is flowing has been the Records of Achievement, promoted by several authorities. These aim to provide a way of supplying all young people with a record of their:

- positive achievements and experiences;
- growth against their own previous standard and against defined knowledge and skills criteria;
- capabilities as a whole person including personal and interpersonal competencies (group and social skills).

This and other like-minded developments will require active learning methods whereby the learners participate in decisions on the nature and pace of what they are doing, and are encouraged to reflect on or evaluate their own learning – individually, with their peers and with staff or other adults in the role of 'critical friends'. Such an approach requires a change in the climate of learning and indeed in the climate of a school.

Above all it requires a change in the status and stance of both teacher and learner. The teacher will need to move away from being a didactic judge of pupils to being a facilitator and enabler of learning. Learners will have more responsibility for their own learning, including in judging their own progress and performance and in contributing to those of their peers. This depends markedly upon changes in staff attitudes and skills. Briefly the main requisites for staff are (as set out in the EEC working paper already referred to):

- To be guides to knowledge rather than sources of it.
- To have non-authoritarian relationships with young people and to accept their participation in decisions.
- To understand the adult world outside the school.
- To understand the competencies young people need.
- To have skills in the use of group and individualized work and in creating learning situations.
- To be able to use the experience of young people as a learning process through reflection.
- To accept that people other than teachers are sources of knowledge and valuable experience.

The trends we have sketched represent a powerful movement away from traditional approaches. They are producing, and will further require, the most fundamental changes within schools, throughout the schooling system at both primary and secondary levels. They need to be addressed by those managing schools – since they affect the 'climate' of a whole school – and by each teacher, since they affect also the 'climate' of learning activities. We have suggested that the product of education is a process of growth within the human being. The basic question is: what are the best ways of producing that process with the young learner in schools? Fundamentally therefore: what is an educated person?

Although no committee would ever have composed Beethoven's fifth symphony, it is also unlikely that any individual could have sent a rocket to the moon. A great deal of human achievement will in future be the result of teamwork.

Wragg, *Classroom Teaching Skills*, 1984

Delivery

Delivery is a question of logistics: how to get the product or service to the customer. Industry and commerce devote a high proportion of time and money to this question. Getting the product to the customer, when, where, how and as it is wanted, is of crucial importance. Why make goods if you are frustrated at the delivery end of the business? In business terms, good road access and links with freight terminals – rail, air and sea-ports – are essential links in a network of delivery systems. This has to reach all outlets to serve the convenience of customers.

But 'convenience' is not a static condition. Customers' habits and expectations change. Greater use of the car has led to 'one-stop shopping' and supermarkets, covered malls, out-of-town centres – but also to pedestrian precincts. New technologies are brought to the aid of the system: computerized stores control and ticket agencies; 24-hour cash dispensers at banks; televised information services; prefabricated components for assembly on site, etc.

In comparison, the delivery of education has stood still. It belongs to the age of the steam railway. To get on the education gravy train you have to attend at a station and can travel only when the trains run – which is usually only for five hours a day during thirty-eight weeks in a year, and never on Saturdays or Sundays! Education is delivered when, where, how and what the *system* decides. Moreover the journey lasts for a year; it has to be started in the autumn and be carried through to the following summer, when at certain times the traveller will get a ticket for transfer to next year's journey.

Why this is so is clear enough and has much to do with the traditions we have inherited. Children must be educated and must attend schools where experts can be assembled to teach them. Those experts are licensed to issue tickets, by way of examination results, to enable the further progress of students. Over the years much has been done to improve this system: in the quality of design of schools, in the qualifications of teachers, in the development of comprehensive education and in examination systems, including the demise of the eleven-plus. But all these developments have been improvements on the design and technology of the original system.

There are many signs that the concepts implicit in that original design are virtually exhausted and will be replaced by other forms of delivery and organization. Schools can no longer claim to be the sole repositories of knowledge, nor can they maintain a position of moated self-sufficiency. The development of information technology is likely to have as revolutionary an effect in the future on school systems as did the invention of printing on the monasteries.

Electronic technology is changing all our communications systems by accelerating the processing, development and delivery of information. Knowledge and facts are being exchanged so rapidly that this is speeding up the development of new knowledge; ideas are outdated more quickly.

Universal access to television, microcomputer links, video recordings and hands-on computerized learning systems, cable TV linked to satellites – all these reduce the dependence upon a teacher to impart knowledge and the need for a learner to attend at an institution to receive that service. 'That colourful box in our living rooms will become an information screen displacing telephone directories, travel agents, estate agents, encyclopaedias and even our daily newspaper' (Stonier).

The effects of this in the schools and the wider education service are already visible. The prime example is the Open University; started in 1969 and now with over 60,000 students, it harnesses television, video and tape recordings with home study kits. Local 'Pick-up' networks have been established using the combined resources of university/polytechnic and further education colleges to provide flexible courses for industry and retraining. Many schools now share their sixth-form work within a consortium. Off-campus resource centres using microcomputers are serving groups of primary and secondary schools. Mobile teams of teachers and technicians are moving between schools or, as in Bedfordshire, taking their 'laboratory' with them in a specially equipped bus.

Computerized language and music laboratories are being developed. Micro-writers, word processors, video recordings, and more sophisticated aids to hearing and visual perception, which particularly help the education of disabled students in mainstream schools, are appearing in schools in increasing numbers. Computers are now in all schools, with more sophisticated programmes enabling 'hands-on' computer-directed interactive learning and computer-assisted design. Increasing numbers of children have access to computers and video recorders at home, and to Prestel, Ceefax and Oracle. 'As these networks expand, the home centre will have information available which vastly exceeds the largest city library' (Stonier). No wonder many young computer whiz-kids have outdistanced their teachers.

The emergence of this electronic technology is changing our capacity of delivering education. It will challenge our traditional forms of organization and it underwrites many of the other trends we have identified. The main features of the new delivery system seem to us to be:

- *Networking*, i.e. education being delivered variously in time, place and method through interconnected networks, including the home.
- *Distance learning*, i.e. learning at a distance from the teacher and school.
- *Independent learning*, using individual computer programmes, which have infinite patience, rely on positive reinforcement and enable

students to monitor their own progress ('It's the first maths teacher that never yelled at me!').

- *Cumulative credit*, i.e. a system whereby learning progress can be credited cumulatively and can be recognized as an interchangeable currency throughout the system.

Where do schools fit into such a system? There must still be a human touch. Children need to be with other children to facilitate their own emotional growth and to develop social skills. 'As computers begin to take over some of the basics of education, schools will more and more be called upon to take responsibility for teaching values and motivation, if not religion' (Naisbitt). The young will still need a framework to facilitate their learning, experiences and activities, and they will need help in organizing and orientating themselves.

Schools will be the knots that hold the net together, using the resources of the network and contributing to it. This will include the resources of the local community and of homes. The curriculum will need to be expressed as a family curriculum. And since education is a lifelong process (and is increasingly seen as such) the school will have its own local network as a drop-in, open-learning, cultural and leisure centre for lifelong education – when, where, how and what people want.

Trends tell you the direction the country is moving in. The decisions are up to you. But trends, like horses, are easier to ride in the direction they are already going. When you make a decision which is compatible with the overarching trend, the trend helps you along. You may decide to buck the trend, but it is still helpful to know it is there.

Naisbitt, *Megatrends*, 1983

The clues to changes

Many of the clues are obvious from what has been said and, indeed, from what has already been happening. Many schools are already responding positively and creatively. But molehills of change are not enough to count as a re-cultivation of the whole field of education; yet that is what is needed, nothing less than a rethinking of the place of the school and the role of the teacher in the development of the individual throughout his or her life. Let us list some of the clues, and the questions they pose for the school.

Market share

The scope of education, as we saw, is increasing. More subjects to learn, more skills to acquire and more years in which to learn them, as lifetime education begins to be taken more literally. Do schools want a declining market share or not? If they stick to teaching their customary subjects to their customary students they will find their market share declining rapidly until they become perhaps the residual institutions for core subjects, working mornings only, maybe, to allow space for others to do the other things that the market will demand. If schools do not take up the kind of curriculum advocated in the EEC working paper we can be sure that others will, be they the agencies of the Department of Employment, the television companies, the computer package makers, parent co-operatives or voluntary agencies (consider, in this light, how the playgroup movement sprang up in reaction to the lack of provision in schools for younger children).

In organizational terms any response to a wider and growing market will mean a more *diversified* organization, geared to more products and more markets. It will mean that the production function (teaching) will have to be tailored much more to what the marketing function wants. The market-place therefore needs to have its representatives inside the organization – more equivalent to product managers co-ordinating parts of the production function to meet specific needs.

If the concept of the market is indeed broadened to include people older than eighteen and skills outside the normal curriculum, then no school can or should attempt to meet all demands. There are, after all, many other delivery institutions, including universities, polytechnics and colleges, that will be part of that growing market. The *strategic* choice for the school must be which parts of the new market it wants to tackle. It needs, however, to be a positive choice not a reluctant drift if the organization is to respond creatively. It is an opportunity for each school to define its own identity more clearly and to specify its chosen purposes more precisely.

In the expanded and developing market it is not clear who will pay for which customers or what products. The educational economy is likely to become more of a mixed economy as every government finds itself unable to meet the growing demands for education. The education system in general, and schools in particular, need to ponder the implications of different sources of payment: part from the state, part from the individuals, part from sponsors. It is a package that higher education in Britain has already learnt to live with; the schools' turn is likely to be next. The result will be more customers with more teeth, and a corresponding need for the school to find a way of keeping in touch with them – product managers again, perhaps?

Product development

New markets need new products. Are schools going to wait until these new products are developed elsewhere for them to use, in councils for curriculum development for example, or in specially funded development units? Or will they start to experiment themselves? Since successful innovation requires a large base of experiments it would be best if schools provided the experimental base, but that means allocating time and resources for product development; it means tolerating the occasional failure and finding the right kind of entrepreneurial spirits among the staff. None of this happens automatically.

Structures

Customized education, more variety in the intake, more distance learning, more consortia – these are all pressures on the model of the school as a self-contained world dominated by a stable role culture. The school will need to re-draw the boundaries of its responsibilities, and these will be very jagged boundaries, moving way beyond the perimeter fence and taking account of outside partners, differing time-blocks and new groupings of children. A role culture will not be able to cope with the complexity. Schools will have to structure themselves much more as a set of interlocking task groups, drawing from the base disciplines, led by enthusiastic team leaders (more product managers?).

Teams, as with much of the rest of the world of work, will dominate the structure, teams with overlapping membership and with project leaders rather than 'heads' in charge. All the truths and dilemmas of groups will become more important. Teams are the building-bricks of networks, and 'network', as we saw, will be the emerging word in education, with the school as the physical, intellectual and managerial centre. But networks are less easy to control or to direct. Power is inevitably given away to the individual teams. No longer will the headteacher be able to look out of the window and see what is going on in the school, because the networks will reach beyond the school. New methods of communication will have to be found, new ways of sharing visions and plans, new ways of checking the performance of staff (by *results* rather than by a feel for their method). Network management after direct rule feels like changing to sail after a power boat; you are dependent on sources of energy that you can use but not determine or initiate, needing sensitivity rather than power, touch instead of force. It is a new art form, a new culture.

Schools will also begin to have a more *federal* structure, one in which several mini-schools are linked together into a confederation. The intention behind federalism is to gain the advantages of scale whilst retaining the identity of smaller units, which are given as much autonomy as possible consistent with remaining linked into the whole. Community schools, which are the first to put their toes into the extended marketplace and to enlarge the time boundaries of the school, can manage the new complexity only by going federal. To telephone such a school and ask for the head is often to get the response, 'Which head?' That is the outward and visible sign of federalism at work.

Within the federal concept more and more groups of students will come to have an identifiable head or form teacher who will share his or her territory with them, using the form as the home-base to which specialists are pulled in and from which the students go out to selected specialities. This system, common as we know in primary schools and the early years of secondary schools, may result in some loss of traditional subject coverage (fewer options) but will increase opportunities for the kind of curriculum advocated by the EEC working paper. Within fixed parameters (of demands and constraints – see Chapter 3) the form teacher will be expected to be the manager of this very mini-school, with much discretion on 'how' to achieve the agreed 'what'.

Output measurement

A more diverse market will need more diverse measurements. Norm-referencing has no point when you can no longer define the population that is providing the norm. Were the GCSE group to include people of all ages, at different stages of development, it would make no sense, in logic or in practice, to use the average as a bench-mark; nor would it be feasible if the examinations were taken at a variety of different times. It is not possible, for example, to norm-reference all driving tests, even though individual examiners carry some implicit 'pass percentage' in their heads.

The likely gradual erosion of fixed age bands for qualifications will do more than anything else to push schools towards criterion-referenced qualifications or other demonstrable proofs of acquired competence – portfolios of experience and achievement. As more such tests get developed it will become easier to provide each student with sets of target objectives with relatively short time-horizons, and with feedback directly related to those targets: each student running against herself or himself in a marathon, rather than looking for one of the rationed top places in the horse-race. Motivation by achievement, rather than by carrot or stick, becomes a real possibility, both for the teacher and for the school head, who will now be better able to judge teachers by their students' progress rather than by subjective impression.

The staff

The role of the teacher, as we have seen, will inevitably change to more that of *agent* than expert, to counsellor and facilitator, manager of learning situations, co-ordinator of projects, team leader or network resource. These are all new words for new roles and consequently have the tinge of jargon, but they signal, like all new words, the need for new behaviours.

To many teachers, accustomed to being the sole authority (representing both the organization and the subject), at least in their own classrooms, the changes will not be easy or comfortable. To others the new patterns of teamwork and shared responsibility will be stimulating and supportive. For some, therefore, there will be even more role ambiguity and possible stress than there is at present. Such people would be best kept out of leadership positions in the network; they would feel more secure and be more useful as resources based in the production function – as subject specialists to be drawn upon by the task teams. What this illustrates is the need for schools to begin to differentiate more between their staff, to identify what each is best at and which culture suits whom rather than to assume that each can do everything.

More roles seem to call for more resources; and resources, whether they be leaders, managers, administrators or teachers, cost money. If the money turns out not to be available the schools will have to be ingenious. But here the new technology may come to their aid. Independent learning, monitored and assisted by computer, may actually imply less student contact time for teachers, releasing more time for the management role, wherever required. Schools may follow other organizations in experimenting with more subcontracting of specialist tasks, paying for specific tasks rather than taking the person on to the payroll; it is cheaper and more flexible for the organization. Other organizations restrict their full-time professional core of key managers and specialists to the minimum, leaving as much as possible to be done by a contractual fringe on specific short-term contracts. Schools may want to go the same way, although they will undoubtedly encounter resistance from the trade unions, more interested as they can be in preserving the status quo than in exploring the future.

Management

A more open, more flexible school will tend to mean more time and resources given to management. Schools would be wise to use the opportunity to distinguish between educational *leadership* and *administration*, along the lines suggested in Chapter 4. The administrators will be required throughout the system but, whilst they must be sensitive to and in tune with the teaching process, they do not themselves have to be professional teachers.

Management, as we have already noted, will become a more prominent feature of school life rather than a poor relation to teaching. It will therefore be taken more seriously and treated more professionally, and may be the preferred career path for many. Every form teacher will be a manager, combining both leadership and administrative functions at that level, and will have to learn to think like a manager – which means developing the kind of understanding described in Chapters 3 and 4 of this book. Where every classroom is an organization in miniature, with its members seen not as the raw material to be processed, or written upon, but as individuals, each one different, working on common and often shared tasks, then the principles of management, not of instruction, come to the fore.

Where will teachers learn these skills? Teacher training, both before and during the teaching career, will surely begin to include more material on management and organizations. Schools may, however, begin to think more radically. If the core roles become those of learning-group managers not subject specialists (who could be confined to the staff roles or even pulled in from the contractual fringe), schools may look for people who have already practised such skills in other organizations. The end of the closed school may mean the end of the closed profession of teaching. That will be threatening to many, but liberating to others.

As we stated at the beginning of this chapter, no one can be sure of the future. Schools may turn their backs on the new opportunities and do only what they know well how to do now, leaving the rest for others.

The federal school may be an impossible dream. Education for everyone anytime may turn out to be too expensive. It is more likely, however, that schools will, in the best British tradition, stumble backwards into the future, looking longingly to the past as they move away from it. If that happens, then the topics discussed in this book will become even more relevant, for the school is bound to be more complicated, and to need more management and a lot more organizational understanding from the student to the head.

References and Further Reading

The principal works referred to in the text are cited here, along with a few other books for those who want to delve deeper into any area. Part Three of *Understanding Organizations* is devoted to short reviews of the literature on each topic. For this reason the list given here is relatively short – it could easily have run to more than three hundred titles!

Most of the references are to works on organization theory; relatively few are to studies of school management. This reflects the bias of this book, which is that we should not think of schools as institutions apart, having little to do with the laws that appear to apply in other organizations. Too many of the books on school management deal almost exclusively with the technicalities of schooling or the administration of schooling; they neglect or take for granted the way individuals behave in different groups, circumstances and structures. Each of the books listed will, however, suggest others in a continuing trail for the interested reader.

AITKEN, R. (1984), 'Education for Autonomy', *RSA Journal*, June. An exposition of an educational philosophy in practice.

ALDERFER, C. P. (1972), *Existence, Relatedness and Growth*, Collier-Macmillan.

BALDWIN, J. and WELLS, H. (1979–83), *Active Tutorial Work*, Books I–VI, Blackwell. A practical and insightful course in social and life skills.

BELBIN, R. M. (1981), *Management Teams: Why They Succeed or Fail*, Heinemann. A very practical study of the mix of roles and characters needed in a successful team.

BUSH, T. *et al.* (eds.) (1980), *Approaches to School Management*, Harper & Row. The Open University Reader, with a cross-section of articles on aspects of school management.

BUTTON, L. (1982), *Development Group Work with Adolescents*, Hodder & Stoughton. A standard work on adolescent groups.

FERGUSON, M. (1981), *The Aquarian Conspiracy: Personal and Social Transformation in the Eighties*, Routledge & Kegan Paul. A special view of the possibilities opening up in society.

GALBRAITH, J. R. (1973), *Designing Complex Organizations*, Addison-Wesley. A good description of the opportunities and problems of the 'matrix' organization.

GUEST, R. K. (1955/6), 'Of Time and the Foreman', *Personnel*, 32.

HANDY, C. (1984), *Taken for Granted? Looking at Schools as Organizations*, Longman. A study, sponsored by the Schools Council, of the organization of schools in the UK.

HANDY, C. (1985), *Understanding Organizations*, 3rd edn, Penguin. An interpretation of the best of the studies and theories in organization theory and behaviour.

HARGREAVES, D. H. (1982), *The Challenge of the Comprehensive School*, Routledge & Kegan Paul. A readable and convincing analysis of the problems and assumptions involved in the way the British do their secondary schooling.

HARRISON, R. (1972), 'How to Describe Your Organization', *Harvard Business Review*, September/October. The original source of the four cultures of organizations.

HERZBERG, F. (1966), *Work and the Nature of Man*, World Publishing. One of the best-known, and most practical, of the motivation theorists.

JANIS, I. (1972), *Victims of Groupthink*, Houghton Mifflin. A provocative account of how groups can go wrong in major historical events.

LEAVITT, H. J. (1978), *Managerial Psychology*, University of Chicago Press. One of the best introductions to behaviour in organizations.

LYONS, G. (1974), *The Administrative Tasks of Head and Senior Teachers in Large Secondary Schools*, University of Bristol. An analysis of how top teachers spend their time in schools.

MCCLELLAND, D. C. (1961), *The Achieving Society*, Van Nostrand.

MACGREGOR BURNS, J. (1978), *Leadership*, Harper & Row. A compendious study of leadership, in politics, war and organizations.

MASLOW, A. H. (1954), *Motivation and Personality*, Harper & Row. The other classic (as well as Herzberg's book) on motivation.

MATTHEW, R. and TONG, S. (1982), *The Role of the Deputy Head in the Comprehensive School*, Ward Lock Education. One of the rare studies of the deputy head and his/her relationship to the management of the school.

MINTZBERG, H. (1973), *The Nature of Managerial Work*, Harper & Row. A lively study of what some chief executives (in business, government and education) actually *do*.

MINTZBERG, H. (1982), *Power In and Around Organizations*, Prentice-Hall. An overview of all that is known or speculated about power in organizations. Massive but useful.

NAISBITT, J. (1983), *Megatrends*, Warner Books. A lively look at North America's (and Britain's) emerging way of life.

PAISEY, A. (1981), *Organization and Management in Schools*, Longmans. A useful and brief introduction to some of the organizational issues in schools.

PETERS, T. J. and WATERMAN, R. H. Jr (1983), *In Search of Excellence*, Harper & Row. The best-selling account of what works well in North American businesses (and schools?).

ROGERS, C. P. (1982), *A Social Psychology of Schooling*, Routledge & Kegan Paul. Required reading for any serious student of motivation in education.

ROGERS, C. (1983), *Freedom to Learn for the Eighties*, Merrill. A classic essay from one of the leaders in learning theory, now revised and updated.

ROSENTHAL, R. and JACOBSON, L. (1968), *Pygmalion in the Classroom*, Holt, Rinehart & Winston. The famous, but controversial, account of the effect of expectations on performance in the classroom.

RUTTER, M. *et al.* (1979), *Fifteen Thousand Hours*, Open Books. A stimulating account of the authors' research into what makes an effective school.

SELANCIK, G. R. and PFEFFER, J. (1977), 'Who Gets Power and How They Hold on to It', *Organizational Dynamics*, Winter. A readable account of how power works in organizations.

STEWART, R. (1983), *Choices for the Manager*, McGraw-Hill. An account of long years of research into the job of a manager (in British organizations), with useful conclusions.

STONIER, T. (1983), *The Wealth of Information*, Thames Methuen. A view of the future in which information and education play a dominant role.

TOFFLER, A. (1976), *Future Shock*, Pan. The popular account of a changing world.

Index

accountability, 31
adult education, 108
adult literacy programme, 108
Alderfer, C. P., 49
all-ability groupings, 24, 28
attribution theory, 55–6
authority:
    bureaucratic control system, 77
    network, 123, 125
    personal control system, 77
    and politics, 81
    sources of, 76
    system of, 77
autocracy, 36–7, 40
autonomy, 36–7

Bacon, Francis, 102
Becker, W. C., 55
behaviour:
    effect of reinforcement on, 55
    standards, 39
Belbin, Meredith, 70
binding organizations, 27
Binet, 110
board of governors, 31
boundaries, 20, 62
Bradford, David, 40–41
bureaucratic control system, 77
Burt, Sir Cyril, 110

career guidance, 30
caretakers, 15
certificating function, 38
change, 102
    facing the future, 102–27
    structural, 95–6
changing values, 109–12

charisma, 75
children, *see* students
club culture, 85–6, 101
    in secondary schools, 93
Cohen, Alan, 40–41
collective purpose, primary schools, 18
Commonwealth immigrants, 105
communication:
    in club cultures, 86
    electronic, 111, 119–20
    new methods, 123
    in role cultures, 87
community, primary schools and, 18–21
Community Education Development Centre, 109
community schools and colleges, 98, 108–9, 124
comprehensive schools:
    all-ability groupings, 28
    autocracy and autonomy in, 37
    ideological control and, 78
    see also secondary schools
computers, 120–21, 122, 125
constraints, 62
contraction, 31, 104
control, 74–83
    authority, 77
    bureaucratic system, 77
    expertise system, 79–80
    ideological, 77–9
    networks, 123, 125
    personal system, 75, 77
    political, 80
    resource power, 74, 75–6
    systems of, 76–83

co-ordination, 99
core units, 96–7
Coventry, 108
crime, juvenile, 106–7
criterion-referenced qualifications,
    124–5
cultures, 83–95
    club cultures, 85–6, 101
    environment and, 92
    history and, 92
    mix of, 91–2
    person culture, 89–90, 93
    role, 86–8, 91, 93–4, 123
    school, 93–5
    size and, 91
    task culture, 88–9, 93, 101
    work flow and, 91–2
cumulative credit, 121
curriculum, prospectuses, 31
custodial functions, 38

decision making groups, 68
delivery, 118–21
demands, choice of roles and, 61–3
Descartes, René, 110
dictatorships, 37
dignity, 71, 115
Disraeli, Benjamin, 110
distance learning, 120
diversity, 98–9

Education Act (1944), 38, 110
ego-ideal, 53–4
Eide, Kjell, 111
electronic technology, 111, 119–20,
    125
employment, changes in, 107
environment, mix of cultures and, 92
equal opportunity, 24, 27, 106
European Economic Community
    (EEC), 105, 116–17, 122, 124
examinations:
    output measurement, 124–5
    Oxford certificate of Educational
        Achievement, 117

school functions, 38
expectancy theory, 51, 56
experience learning, 29
expert power, 75, 79–80

falling rolls, 31–2, 104
false economy, 100–101
families:
    changing patterns of, 106
    relationship with primary schools,
        18–19
    relationship with secondary
        schools, 30
federal structure, 124, 127
finance, falling rolls and, 32
Fletcher, Colin, 109
form teachers, 124, 126
forward planning, 102–27
Fromm, Erich, 112
function of schools, 38–40, 71
funds, see finance
future predictions, 102–27

games, organizational, 82
goals:
    motivation, 51–3
    over-arching, 40
    of school education, 39–40
governors, 31
group teaching, 64
groups:
    balanced, 70
    decision making, 68
    forming, 67
    handling, 47
    individuals in, 47, 63–71
    leadership, 68–9
    norming, 68
    performing, 68
    process of, 67–9
    purposes, 65–6, 71
    roles in, 69–71
    size, 65, 66–7
    storming, 67

theories of, 47
Guest, R. K., 41

handicapped children, 105
Handy, C., 84, 93
Hargreaves, David, 71, 115
Harrison, Roger, 84
head teachers:
  autocracy, 36
  giving staff responsibilities, 17–18
  primary school organization, 16–18
  relationships, 16–18
Hemmings, James, 111
Hertzberg, F., 49
Houghton Report, 35
house systems, 28
human rights legislation, 106

identity, with organizations, 28
ideology, control systems, 77–9
independent learning, 120–21
individualism, 71, 110
individuals:
  attribution theory, 55–6
  dealing with, 47–72
  expectancy theory, 56
  goal theories, 51–3
  in groups, 47, 63–71
  as individuals, 47–57
  need theories, 49–51
  reinforcement theory, 54–5
  in roles, 47, 57–63
  self theories, 53–6
influence:
  authority and, 77
  systems of, 76–83
information technology, 111, 119–20, 125
innovation, funding for, 32

Jacobson, L., 56
Janis, I., 67
job-shop structure, primary schools, 14
juvenile crime, 106–7

Lawrence, 27
leadership:
  and administration, 126
  and falling rolls, 31–2
  groups, 68–9
  roles, 17
  see also control; managers
leaving age, 104–5
Leavitt, H. J., 100
leisure activities, 108
Locke, John, 110
Lorsch, 27
Lyons, Geoffrey, 36, 60–61

McClelland, D. C., 49, 50
MacGregor Burns, J., 83
Madsen, C. H., 55
management, future trends, 126
managers:
  activities, 36
  choice of roles, 61
  needs theory of motivation, 50
  roles of, 60–61
  teachers as, 34–8, 44–5
  teachers as natural, 41–3
  work fragmentation, 36, 41, 60
Manpower Services Commission, 102, 105
market, future predictions, 103–12
market research, 102–3
market share, 122–3
Maslow, A. H., 49
Matthew, Richard, 94
measurement of success, 39
meeting-rooms, 35
meetings, timing of, 35
Mintzberg, H., 41, 76, 81, 82
money, see finance
morality, 39
Morris, Henry, 108
motivation, 125
  within organizations, 28
motivation theory, 47, 49–57
  attribution theory, 55–6
  expectancy theory, 56

motivation theory—*continued*
  goal theories, 51–3
  need theories, 49–51
  reinforcement theory, 54–5
  self theories, 53–6

Naisbitt, John, 115, 121
need theories of motivation, 49–51
negative power, 81
networking, 120
networks, 123–4

OCEA, *see* Oxford Certificate of
  Education Achievement
offices, lack of managerial, 35
Open University, 120
operational research, 102–3
organization:
  games, 82
  primary schools, 14–16
  secondary schools, 23–9
organizations:
  boundaries, 20
  club culture, 85–6
  core units, 96–7
  cultural mix, 91–2
  differentiation, 27
  groups and, 57
  individual's role within, 27–8
  person culture and, 89–90
  politics, 80–83
  professional, 41–2
  role culture and, 86–8
  roles and, 57
  running, 73–101
  splitting and binding, 27
  structuring, 95–101
  system of expertise and, 79–80
  task cultures, 88–9
output measurement, 124–5
outside experience, 29
over-arching goals, 40
Oxford Certificate of Education
  Achievement (OCEA), 117

parents:
  information about schools, 31
  primary schools and, 18–21
  relationships with secondary
    schools, 30
  say in education, 106
pastoral care, secondary schools,
  28–9
paternalism, 110
path–goal theory, 51
Peabody, 76
performance review, 53
person cultures, 89–90
  teachers as, 93
personal power, 75
personality conflict, 17
Peters, T. J., 33
Piaget, J., 98
playgroup movement, 122
political control, 80–83
position power, 74, 75–6
power, 74–83
  expert power, 75, 79–80
  networks, 123
  personal, 75
  position power, 74, 75–6
  resource power, 74, 75–6
  see also control
primary schools, 13–21
  autocracy and autonomy in, 37
  collective purpose, 18
  and the community, 18–21
  co-ordination, 99
  core units, 96
  cultures in, 93, 94
  moving on to secondary schools,
    44
  organization, 14–16
  parents and, 18–21
  reinforcement in the classroom, 55
  relationships, 16–18
  roles and responsibilities, 17–18
problem-solving, task cultures and,
  89
product development, 123

product of education, 112–18
professional organizations, 42
    person culture and, 89–90
professionalism, 79–80, 94
promotion structure, 41
prospectuses, 31, 106
psychological contracts, 47–8, 56–7
public disorder, 106
pupils, *see* students
purpose, in groups, 71

qualifications, criterion-referenced,
    124–5

reinforcement in the classroom, 55
reinforcement theory, 54–5
relationships:
    primary schools, 16–18
    secondary schools, 29–30
Rennie, John, 109
research, 102–3
resource power, 74, 75–6
resources, future needs, 125, 126
rituals, 77–8
Rogers, Carl, 116
role ambiguity, 58, 63, 125
    reducing, 42–3, 60
    in teachers, 42
role conflict, 58–9, 60, 100
role culture, 86–8, 91, 123
    teaching as, 93
role overload, 59, 60, 100
role strain, 59–60
role-switching, 41–3
role theory, 47
role underload, 59
roles:
    choice in, 61–3
    in groups, 69–71
    individuals in, 57–63
    managerial, 60–61
    new, 95
    problems in, 58
Rosenthal, R., 56
Rutter, M., 63

Scarman Report, 106
school-leaving age, 104–5
Secondary Heads' Association, 100
secondary schools, 21–30
    all-ability groupings, 24, 28
    autocracy and autonomy in, 37
    as community colleges, 108
    core units, 96–7
    differentiation, 26–7
    external relationships, 30
    individualism, 71
    moving up to, 44
    organization, 23–9
    pastoral care, 28–9
    relationships, 29–30
    role culture in, 93–4
    size, 22
    student organization, 44–5
self theories:
    attribution theory, 55–6
    expectancy theory, 56
    of motivation, 53–7
    reinforcement theory, 54–5
self-confidence, 54
self-esteem, 53–6
shared values, 33
sixth forms, organization, 44
size:
    groups, 65, 66–7
    mix of cultures and, 91
    of schools, 22
socialization, 77
socializing functions, 39
society, schools and, 31–2
Spearman, 110
splitting organizations, 27
staffing ratios, secondary schools, 22
Stewart, Rosemary, 36, 41, 61
Stonier, T., 120
stress, role ambiguity and, 42
structuring organizations, 95–101
    co-ordination, 99
    core units, 96–7
    diversity, 98–9
    false economy, 100–101

structuring organizations—*continued*
  structural change, 95–6
  territory, 97
students:
  falling rolls, 31–2, 104
  new groups of, 107–9
  new needs of, 105–7
  and organization, 43–5
  relationship with school and
    community, 20–21
  role underload, 59
  teachers' relationship with, 113–18
  traditional, 104–5
subcontracting, specialist tasks, 125
subject specialization, 24, 25–6
success measurement, 39
Sutton, Ashfield, 109
symbols, 77–87

task culture, 88–9, 101
  teachers and, 92, 94
task groups, 29
teachers:
  choice of roles, 61–2
  contracts, 35
  cultures, 93–5
  and electronic technology, 111,
    119–20
  and experience teaching, 29
  federal structure, 124
  form, 124
  future role, 123, 125–6
  goal theories, 52
  and groups, 63–71
  leadership roles, 17, 126

  as managers, 35–8, 44–5, 126
  as natural managers, 41–3
  needs theories of motivation, 50
  parents and, 19–21
  pastoral care, 29
  performance reviews, 53
  primary school organization, 14–16
  professionalism, 79–80, 94
  promotion structure, 41
  relationship with students, 113–18
  relationships in secondary schools,
    29–30
  role ambiguity, 42
  role switching, 42–3
  selection, 37
  staffing ratios, 22
  training, 126
teams, 123
territory, 97
Thomas, D. R., 55
Toffler, Alvin, 106
Tong, Simon, 94
trade unions, 94

unemployment, 107
UNESCO, 109

Warnock Committee, 105
Waterman, R. H., 33
Webb, P. C., 60–61
work-flow, mix of cultures and, 91–2
Wragg, 118

Youth Service, 108

FOR THE BEST IN PAPERBACKS, LOOK FOR THE

In every corner of the world, on every subject under the sun, Penguin represents quality and variety – the very best in publishing today.

For complete information about books available from Penguin – including Puffins, Penguin Classics and Arkana – and how to order them, write to us at the appropriate address below. Please note that for copyright reasons the selection of books varies from country to country.

In the United Kingdom: Please write to *Dept E.P., Penguin Books Ltd, Harmondsworth, Middlesex, UB7 0DA.*

If you have any difficulty in obtaining a title, please send your order with the correct money, plus ten per cent for postage and packaging, to *PO Box No 11, West Drayton, Middlesex*

In the United States: Please write to *Dept BA, Penguin, 299 Murray Hill Parkway, East Rutherford, New Jersey 07073*

In Canada: Please write to *Penguin Books Canada Ltd, 2801 John Street, Markham, Ontario L3R 1B4*

In Australia: Please write to the *Marketing Department, Penguin Books Australia Ltd, P.O. Box 257, Ringwood, Victoria 3134*

In New Zealand: Please write to the *Marketing Department, Penguin Books (NZ) Ltd, Private Bag, Takapuna, Auckland 9*

In India: Please write to *Penguin Overseas Ltd, 706 Eros Apartments, 56 Nehru Place, New Delhi, 110019*

In the Netherlands: Please write to *Penguin Books Netherlands B.V., Postbus 195, NL–1380AD Weesp*

In West Germany: Please write to *Penguin Books Ltd, Friedrichstrasse 10–12, D–6000 Frankfurt/Main 1*

In Spain: Please write to *Longman Penguin España, Calle San Nicolas 15, E–28013 Madrid*

In Italy: Please write to *Penguin Italia s.r.l., Via Como 4, I-20096 Pioltello (Milano)*

In France: Please write to *Penguin Books Ltd, 39 Rue de Montmorency, F-75003 Paris*

In Japan: Please write to *Longman Penguin Japan Co Ltd, Yamaguchi Building, 2–12–9 Kanda Jimbocho, Chiyoda-Ku, Tokyo 101*

FOR THE BEST IN PAPERBACKS, LOOK FOR THE 🐧

PENGUIN SCIENCE AND MATHEMATICS

Facts from Figures   M. J. Moroney

Starting from the very first principles of the laws of chance, this authoritative 'conducted tour of the statistician's workshop' provides an essential introduction to the major techniques and concepts used in statistics today.

God and the New Physics   Paul Davies

Can science, now come of age, offer a surer path to God than religion? This 'very interesting' (*New Scientist*) book suggests it can.

Descartes' Dream   Philip J. Davis and Reuben Hersh

All of us are 'drowning in digits' and depend constantly on mathematics for our high-tech lifestyle. But is so much mathematics really good for us? This major book takes a sharp look at the ethical issues raised by our computerized society.

The Blind Watchmaker   Richard Dawkins

'An enchantingly witty and persuasive neo-Darwinist attack on the anti-evolutionists, pleasurably intelligible to the scientifically illiterate' – Hermione Lee in the *Observer* Books of the Year

Microbes and Man   John Postgate

From mining to wine-making, microbes play a crucial role in human life. This clear, non-specialist book introduces us to microbes in all their astounding versatility – and to the latest and most exciting developments in microbiology and immunology.

Asimov's New Guide to Science   Isaac Asimov

A classic work brought up to date – far and away the best one-volume survey of all the physical and biological sciences.

FOR THE BEST IN PAPERBACKS, LOOK FOR THE 🐧

PENGUIN PSYCHOLOGY

Introduction to Jung's Psychology   Frieda Fordham

'She has delivered a fair and simple account of the main aspects of my psychological work. I am indebted to her for this admirable piece of work' – C. G. Jung in the Foreword

Child Care and the Growth of Love   John Bowlby

His classic 'summary of evidence of the effects upon children of lack of personal attention ... it presents to administrators, social workers, teachers and doctors a reminder of the significance of the family' – *The Times*

The Anatomy of Human Destructiveness   Erich Fromm

What makes men kill? How can we explain man's lust for cruelty and destruction? 'If any single book could bring mankind to its senses, this book might qualify for that miracle' – Lewis Mumford

Sanity, Madness and the Family   R. D. Laing and A. Esterson

Schizophrenia: fact or fiction? Certainly not fact, according to the authors of this controversial book. Suggesting that some forms of madness may be largely social creations, *Sanity, Madness and the Family* demands to be taken very seriously indeed.

The Social Psychology of Work   Michael Argyle

Both popular and scholarly, Michael Argyle's classic account of the social factors influencing our experience of work examines every area of working life – and throws constructive light on potential problems.

Check Your Own I.Q.   H. J. Eysenck

The sequel to his controversial bestseller, containing five new standard (omnibus) tests and three specifically designed tests for verbal, numerical and visual–spatial ability.

FOR THE BEST IN PAPERBACKS, LOOK FOR THE 🐧

PENGUIN PSYCHOLOGY

Psychoanalysis and Feminism   Juliet Mitchell

'Juliet Mitchell has risked accusations of apostasy from her fellow feminists. Her book not only challenges orthodox feminism, however; it defies the conventions of social thought in the English-speaking countries ... a brave and important book' – *New York Review of Books*

Helping Troubled Children   Michael Rutter

Written by a leading practitioner and researcher in child psychiatry, a full and clear account of the many problems encountered by young school-age children – development, emotional disorders, underachievement – and how they can be given help.

The Divided Self   R. D. Laing

'A study that makes all other works I have read on schizophrenia seem fragmentary ... The author brings, through his vision and perception, that particular touch of genius which causes one to say "Yes, I have always known that, why have I never thought of it before?"' – *Journal of Analytical Psychology*

The Origins of Religion   Sigmund Freud

The thirteenth volume in the *Penguin Freud Library* contains Freud's views on the subject of religious belief – including *Totem and Taboo*, regarded by Freud as his best-written work.

The Informed Heart   Bruno Bettelheim

Bettelheim draws on his experience in concentration camps to illuminate the dangers inherent in all mass societies in this profound and moving masterpiece.

Introducing Social Psychology   Henri Tajfel and Colin Fraser (eds.)

From evolutionary changes to the social influence processes in a given group, a distinguished team of contributors demonstrate how our interaction with others and our views of the social world shape and modify much of what we do.

FOR THE BEST IN PAPERBACKS, LOOK FOR THE 🐧

PENGUIN LANGUAGE/LINGUISTICS

Sociolinguistics   Peter Trudgill

Women speak 'better' English than men. The Eskimo language has several words for snow. 1001 factors influence the way we speak; Professor Trudgill draws on languages from Afrikaans to Yiddish to illuminate this fascinating topic and provide a painless introduction to sociolinguistics.

The English Language   David Crystal

A guided tour of the language by the presenter of BBC Radio 4's *English Now*: the common structures that unify the language; the major variations from Ireland to the Caribbean; the 'dialects' of chemists and clergy, lawyers and truckers.

Semantics   Geoffrey Leech

'Integrated, coherent and stimulating ... discusses all the important current issues in semantics' – *Language in Society*

Our Language   Simeon Potter

'The author is brilliantly successful in his effort to instruct by delighting ... he contrives not only to give a history of English but also to talk at his ease on rhyming slang, names, spelling reform, American English and much else ... fascinating' – *Higher Education Journal*

Grammar   Frank Palmer

In modern linguistics grammar means far more than cases, tenses and declensions – it means precise and scientific description of the structure of language. This concise guide takes the reader simply and clearly through the concepts of traditional grammar, morphology, sentence structure and transformational–generative grammar.

Linguistics   David Crystal

Phonetics, phonology and morphology, 'surface' and 'deep' syntax, semantics and pragmatics ... A novel and lively introduction to a subject which today concerns not only psychologists, sociologists and philosophers but teachers, interpreters and even telephone companies.

FOR THE BEST IN PAPERBACKS, LOOK FOR THE 🐧

PENGUIN POLITICS AND SOCIAL SCIENCES

Political Ideas David Thomson (ed.)

From Machiavelli to Marx – a stimulating and informative introduction to the last 500 years of European political thinkers and political thought.

On Revolution Hannah Arendt

Arendt's classic analysis of a relatively recent political phenomenon examines the underlying principles common to all revolutions, and the evolution of revolutionary theory and practice. 'Never dull, enormously erudite, always imaginative' – *Sunday Times*

The Apartheid Handbook Roger Omond

The facts behind the headlines: the essential hard information about how apartheid actually works from day to day.

The Social Construction of Reality Peter Berger and Thomas Luckmann

Concerned with the sociology of 'everything that passes for knowledge in society' and particularly with that which passes for common sense, this is 'a serious, open-minded book, upon a serious subject' – *Listener*

The Care of the Self Michel Foucault
The History of Sexuality Vol 3

Foucault examines the transformation of sexual discourse from the Hellenistic to the Roman world in an inquiry which 'bristles with provocative insights into the tangled liaison of sex and self' – *The Times Higher Educational Supplement*

A Fate Worse than Debt Susan George

How did Third World countries accumulate a staggering trillion dollars' worth of debt? Who really shoulders the burden of reimbursement? How should we deal with the debt crisis? Susan George answers these questions with the solid evidence and verve familiar to readers of *How the Other Half Dies*.

FOR THE BEST IN PAPERBACKS, LOOK FOR THE

PENGUIN POLITICS AND SOCIAL SCIENCES

Comparative Government S. E. Finer

'A considerable *tour de force* ... few teachers of politics in Britain would fail to learn a great deal from it ... Above all, it is the work of a great teacher who breathes into every page his own enthusiasm for the discipline' – Anthony King in *New Society*

Karl Marx: Selected Writings in Sociology and Social Philosophy
T. B. Bottomore and Maximilien Rubel (eds.)

'It makes available, in coherent form and lucid English, some of Marx's most important ideas. As an introduction to Marx's thought, it has very few rivals indeed' – *British Journal of Sociology*

Post-War Britain A Political History Alan Sked and Chris Cook

Major political figures from Attlee to Thatcher, the aims and achievements of governments and the changing fortunes of Britain in the period since 1945 are thoroughly scrutinized in this readable history.

Inside the Third World Paul Harrison

From climate and colonialism to land hunger, exploding cities and illiteracy, this comprehensive book brings home a wealth of facts and analysis on the often tragic realities of life for the poor people and communities of Asia, Africa and Latin America.

Housewife Ann Oakley

'A fresh and challenging account' – *Economist*. 'Informative and rational enough to deserve a serious place in any discussion on the position of women in modern society' – *The Times Educational Supplement*

The Raw and the Cooked Claude Lévi-Strauss

Deliberately, brilliantly and inimitably challenging, Lévi-Strauss's seminal work of structural anthropology cuts wide and deep into the mind of mankind, as he finds in the myths of the South American Indians a comprehensible psychological pattern.